How to Stop

E-MAIL SPAM, SPYWARE, MALWARE, COMPUTER VIRUSES, AND HACKERS

From Ruining Your Computer Or Network

The Complete Guide For Your Home And Work

By Bruce C. Brown

HOW TO STOP E-MAIL SPAM, SPYWARE, MALWARE, COMPUTER VIRUSES, AND HACKERS FROM RUINING YOUR COMPUTER OR NETWORK: THE COMPLETE GUIDE FOR YOUR HOME AND WORK

Library of Congress Cataloging-in-Publication Data

Brown, Bruce C. (Bruce Cameron), 1965-
  How to stop e-mail spam, spyware, malware, computer viruses, and hackers from ruining your computer or network : the complete guide for your home and work / by Bruce C. Brown.
       p. cm.
  Includes bibliographical references and index.
  ISBN-13: 978-1-60138-303-7 (alk. paper)
  ISBN-10: 1-60138-303-7 (alk. paper)
  1. Computer security. 2. Computer networks--Security measures. 3. Malware (Computer software)--Prevention. I. Title.
   QA76.9.A25B7748 2010
   005.8--dc22
                                    2010009332

All trademarks, trade names, or logos mentioned or used are the property of their respective owners and are used only to directly describe the products being provided. Every effort has been made to properly capitalize, punctuate, identify, and attribute trademarks and trade names to their respective owners, including the use of ® and ™ wherever possible and practical. Atlantic Publishing Group, Inc. is not a partner, affiliate, or licensee with the holders of said trademarks.

LIMIT OF LIABILITY/DISCLAIMER OF WARRANTY: The publisher and the author make no representations or warranties with respect to the accuracy or completeness of the contents of this work and specifically disclaim all warranties, including without limitation warranties of fitness for a particular purpose. No warranty may be created or extended by sales or promotional materials. The advice and strategies contained herein may not be suitable for every situation. This work is sold with the understanding that the publisher is not engaged in rendering legal, accounting, or other professional services. If professional assistance is required, the services of a competent professional should be sought. Neither the publisher nor the author shall be liable for damages arising herefrom. The fact that an organization or Web site is referred to in this work as a citation and/or a potential source of further information does not mean that the author or the publisher endorses the information the organization or Web site may provide or recommendations it may make. Further, readers should be aware that Internet Web sites listed in this work may have changed or disappeared between when this work was written and when it is read.

Printed in the United States

PROJECT MANAGER: MELISSA PETERSON • EDITORIAL ASSISTANT: KATY DOLL
EDITORIAL ASSISTANT: BRAD GOLDBACH • FREELANCE EDITOR: REBECCA BENTZ
PEER REVIEW: MARILEE GRIFFIN • INTERIOR DESIGN: RHANA GITTENS
FRONT & BACK COVER DESIGN: JACKIE MILLER • MILLERJACKIEJ@GMAIL.COM

Printed on Recycled Paper

We recently lost our beloved pet "Bear," who was not only our best and dearest friend but also the "Vice President of Sunshine" here at Atlantic Publishing. He did not receive a salary but worked tirelessly 24 hours a day to please his parents. Bear was a rescue dog that turned around and showered myself, my wife, Sherri, his grandparents Jean, Bob, and Nancy, and every person and animal he met (maybe not rabbits) with friendship and love. He made a lot of people smile every day.

We wanted you to know that a portion of the profits of this book will be donated to The Humane Society of the United States. *–Douglas & Sherri Brown*

The human-animal bond is as old as human history. We cherish our animal companions for their unconditional affection and acceptance. We feel a thrill when we glimpse wild creatures in their natural habitat or in our own backyard.

Unfortunately, the human-animal bond has at times been weakened. Humans have exploited some animal species to the point of extinction.

The Humane Society of the United States makes a difference in the lives of animals here at home and worldwide. The HSUS is dedicated to creating a world where our relationship with animals is guided by compassion. We seek a truly humane society in which animals are respected for their intrinsic value, and where the human-animal bond is strong.

Want to help animals? We have plenty of suggestions. Adopt a pet from a local shelter, join The Humane Society and be a part of our work to help companion animals and wildlife. You will be funding our educational, legislative, investigative and outreach projects in the U.S. and across the globe.

Or perhaps you'd like to make a memorial donation in honor of a pet, friend or relative? You can through our Kindred Spirits program. And if you'd like to contribute in a more structured way, our Planned Giving Office has suggestions about estate planning, annuities, and even gifts of stock that avoid capital gains taxes.

Maybe you have land that you would like to preserve as a lasting habitat for wildlife. Our Wildlife Land Trust can help you. Perhaps the land you want to share is a backyard—that's enough. Our Urban Wildlife Sanctuary Program will show you how to create a habitat for your wild neighbors.

So you see, it's easy to help animals. And The HSUS is here to help.

2100 L Street NW • Washington, DC 20037 • 202-452-1100
www.hsus.org

DEDICATION

I looked back at my ten previous books and discovered that I had dedicated six of them to my wife! Well, who better to dedicate a book to than the person who has stuck with me for more than 25 years; endured countless moves across the country; spent too many nights home alone while I was deployed, underway, or traveling; and put up with all my annoying habits? Thanks for hanging in there — I could not have done any of this without you!

TABLE OF CONTENTS

CHAPTER 2: Computer Viruses: Are You at Risk? 43

CHAPTER 3: Antivirus Solutions & Defense 63

CHAPTER 4: Spam, Spoofing, Phishing, & E-Mail Hoaxes: What They Are and How to Block Them 83

CHAPTER 5: Detecting and Countering Malware & Spyware   121

CHAPTER 6: Web Browsers, Pop-Up Windows, & How to Surf the Web Safely 153

CHAPTER 7: Firewalls: A Comprehensive Introduction 165

CHAPTER 8: Hackers: How to Defend Against Hacks & Other Attacks 185

CHAPTER 9: Network Security: How to Protect and Secure your Home or Small-business Network 199

CHAPTER 10: Wireless Network Security: How to Secure Your Wireless Network 223

CHAPTER 11: Software Products to Protect Your Computers & Networks   251

CONCLUSION   273

GLOSSARY   277

AUTHOR BIOGRAPHY   283

BIBLIOGRAPHY   285

INDEX   287

FOREWORD

Today, we live in a hyper-connected society fueled in large part by the Internet. As everyday users, we conduct most of our daily tasks online: from work-related research and online banking to e-mailing and social networking.

The Internet may be a limitless playground of information, but despite all the advantages it offers, it also introduces a number of risks that can damage not only our computers, but our daily lives. In fact, an entire industry of cyber criminals is making millions of dollars off innocent Web users. These cyber criminals work day in and day out developing new invasive and silent malware crafted to give them complete control of our computers and all of our most personal data.

Although you might only hear about the highest profile attacks in the media, the reality is that there are much less publicized, yet incredibly dangerous, threats on the Web every day, and you can be just a click away from being affected. One example is BlackHat SEO attacks, which are criminally motivated search engine optimization schemes designed to tie malicious URLs to breaking news content. In a BlackHat SEO attack, simply searching for any breaking news topic in your favorite search engine can land you at the front step of cyber criminals' doors, leaving your computer infected and your data unprotected.

Personal users and small business owners are those most at risk of falling victims to attacks, often navigating the Web without updated firewalls and antivirus software. Small businesses, which typically have limited in-house resources and IT staffs to dedicate to security, have particularly become attractive cyber criminal targets. In a recent study conducted by PandaLabs, we found that 44 percent of more than 1,400 surveyed small- to medium-sized businesses in the United States admitted to falling victim to cyber crime.

Home users and businesses should be concerned. Malware on the Web continues to grow exponentially as criminals are becoming increasingly financially motivated. In 2009, PandaLabs, the malware analysis and detection laboratory I work for, detected and classified more than 25 million malware samples within its cloud computing database, 66 percent of which were malicious Trojans designed to steal banking data and personal information. In PandaLabs' most recent study on the rise of rogueware, we concluded that cyber criminals were making up to $34 million dollars per month with their extortion-schemed malware designed to scare users into purchasing fake security software.

With millions of computers operating without any protection or outdated security software, and many users unaware of safe Internet browsing practices, cyber criminals have been perpetrating their scams with little difficulty and have been able to make a living off their crimes.

Governments are currently in the infancy stages of drafting cyber security initiatives strong enough to enforce laws on local, state, and international levels, but it is still up to consumers to proactively protect themselves against cyber attacks.

Reading this book is a great first step in getting up to speed on security threats and how to protect yourself, your family, and if you are a business owner, your company. Author Bruce C. Brown lays out each chapter in easy-to-read segments, so that by the end, you will not only understand the terminology and various attack vectors, but will be armed with a wealth of knowledge about which tools you can start using today to ward off cyber criminals.

Sean-Paul Correll is a threat researcher at PandaLabs, the malware analysis and detection laboratory for Panda Security. Correll is credited with discovering the Twitter trending topics attacks, as well as for leading groundbreaking research on social networking cyber crime and BlackHat SEO. Correll serves as a frequent resource for national and security press, including USA Today, PC World, Computerworld, InformationWeek, and many others. He is also the founder of the Malware Database, a repository of malware information that aids fellow researchers in sharing malware samples and threat intelligence. He recently spoke at Security B-Sides Las Vegas and is a frequent contributor to ISSA's events and publications.

www.pandasecurity.com
http://pandalabs.pandasecurity.com/

Address:
Panda Security
230 N. Maryland Avenue 303
Glendale, CA 91206

INTRODUCTION

S pam, spyware, malware, phishing, hacking, and other threats to your home and business computers are very real and can be extraordinarily damaging. Millions of dollars and many work days are lost each year dealing with damage and casualty control caused by these active threats. Although attacks on government computer systems make the news on a regular basis, the truth is home and small business computers are the targets of the majority of attempts to break through computers' defenses on a daily basis. Every computer is a potential target and must be protected against these threats.

What if you lost all the data on your home or business computers? Think of the amount of software, documents, music, photographs, financial records, and more that could be instantly destroyed, stolen, or exploited. Identity theft is a very real threat and securing your personal data is critical to protecting your interests. Personally identifiable information (PII) is information that identifies who you are and might contain home addresses, social security numbers, phone numbers, bank account information, and more. This information, in the hands of a hacker, could wield incredible damage on your personal life and might destroy your business. You must protect your home and business computer systems and networks against current and future threats and use common sense in developing and deploying your lines of defense against these intruders. Something as seemingly harmless as an e-mail with a small attachment has the capability of destroying your computer system or network. Even if you are one the few people who regularly back up data, the loss of a computer to a virus or hacker can have an immense financial toll, not to mention the time and effort it takes to rebuild your systems, reinstall software, and restore data.

Luckily, you can easily defend yourself against most of these threats and successfully protect yourself against would be intruders. This book will help you to ensure that you have protected yourself and your home and business computers and networks, and ensure you have deployed the right tools to secure your data. This book, similar to my previous books, is written for the home user or small business owner who does not have a dedicated technology department or a large information technology budget to procure advanced virus, spyware, and network protection systems. Unbelievably, you can fully protect your computer or network for little money and in many instances for no money at all. We will discuss various options in depth as we break down each topic area by chapter and provide you with detailed plans and various low- or no-cost options to protect you from the thousands of active threats on the Internet. This book is not intended to be technically challenging and the average home computer user should be able to easily understand the concepts in it and protect valuable investments and data.

The goal of a hacker or computer attacker is very simple and primarily based on economics. You have valuable data, secure access to financial records, financial accounts, and personally identifiable information they want. They want this information for their economic gain, to use this information illegally to make money. Other incentives might simply be to inflict damage or harm upon the recipient of the attack, disrupt services or commerce, destroy data, reduce computer or network functionality, and disrupt your personal or business lifestyle. Although there are many other reasons and motivations behind malware and other cyber crimes, remember, it usually comes down to monetary gain.

The following is just a short list of some of the most prolific threats we face today on the Internet, each of which we will discuss further in this book:

- **Computer viruses** are programs that attack your computer, disrupt your network, and steal or destroy your data files. Typically received by e-mail or transmitted through portable storage devices (such as flash drives), they can attack home computers or large network computer systems.

- **Spyware** is software that steals information from your computer and sends it somewhere else. Typically stolen information is financial data, personally identifying information, and computer data files, keystrokes, or passwords.

- **Spoofing** occurs when another computer or network appears to be a "trusted" source when in fact it is not. As with spyware, spoofing attempts to gain unauthorized access to computers and networks to steal or destroy data.

- **Trojans** — or Trojan horses — are software programs whose sole purpose is to damage, disrupt, or destroy computer systems and networks. The effect of this can be wide-ranging from lost or destroyed data to the hijacking of your computers and networks by a third party, where you lose control over your own computer system.

- **Spam** is something we are all familiar with, and though many consider it just a mild nuisance, it is in fact a form of attack on your computer system. Spam is often associated with viruses or offensive or sexually oriented material and can overwhelm Web mail and exchange servers. Spoofed e-mails typically generate hundreds of thousands of spam e-mails that may appear to come from your e-mail account, even though you did not send the e-mails.

- **Adware**, although similar to spyware is typically not destructive in nature, in that it is not intended to damage your computer system. Instead, adware loads your browser, desktop, and system with junk advertisements. These can be hard to battle, because they might "spawn" relentlessly as you close out a browser window; several more might spontaneously open, over and over again. Adware is transmitted through e-mail, instant messengers, and illicit Web sites. If you are still in the minority of Internet users who use dial-up modems, dialers can redirect your modem phone numbers from your normal service provider typically overseas, resulting in enormous phone bills.

- **Hijacking** occurs when a software application takes control of your Web browser, forcing you to navigate to pages you do not want to visit. These sites are typically pornographic in nature or automatically download spyware, adware, and more. Hackers are individuals — with the assistance of software and/or hardware — who attempt to break through your firewall and network security to steal your personal data, financial records, and passwords. Some are more malicious than others and might destroy data, your network, and much more.

- **Phishing** has become very prevalent and is often hard to detect. These e-mails appear to be from reputable sources, such as PayPal, banks, credit unions, and eBay. Often they are written to compel you to log in, with language such as "fraud was detected on your account; please log in immediately to validate your current charges." The embedded URL in these e-mails does not take you to the trusted Web site; instead, it takes you to a fake site in an attempt to get you to log in so phishers can steal your user name and password. They then take your information (such as a PayPal user name and password), log into your PayPal account, change your password so you cannot log in, and then transfer your money out of your account.

- **Hoaxes** are e-mails you receive from people such as the deposed king of Nigeria, who has $20 million in an offshore account and needs you to help him get it out of the country into your account. For your cooperation, you will get a handsome 10 percent of the total. You give away your account information so they can move the money into your account, and magically, your account is drained of every cent you had in it. This is a hoax and people fall for it every single day, sometimes over and over again. Leave yourself unprotected and you will be the victim of some form of attack — guaranteed.

This book will break down and tackle each of the above threats in depth, arming you with the weapons you need to protect your identity, computer systems, and critical data.

You might wonder why you need this book. There are many other books written about viruses, hackers, and computer security; however, most of them are out of date, incredibly complex, and cover only one subject from the wide array of malware threats we face today. This book does not provide you with useless technical information or the history of viruses. This book does not cover only one form of malware, leaving you wondering about how to deal with the rest. This book is your handy reference to the world of malware and online threats, and is packed with all the information you need to secure and protect your computers and networks on the modern Internet.

Is This Book for Me?

This book is written for anyone who uses the Internet; owns computers; has a personal network, a wireless network, business computers, or a business network; stores data on computers; and accesses secure Web sites. It is for the home user, small business, large business, and sole proprietor. If you use a computer, have data stored on a hard drive, access the Internet, or access a network, this book is for you. This book will help you protect your personal data, as well as corporate data. It will give you the background and detailed explanations of what threats exist today, how to identify them, how to combat them, how to protect your data, how to protect your privacy, and how to ensure you are never a victim of a malicious attack. You can easily and effectively protect your computer, network, and critical data; this book will show you how and give you recommendations and guidance for how to do it for little or no money.

This book is primarily written for Windows-based personal computers and covers all versions through Windows 7. In general, Macintosh computers are less prone to viruses, hacking, and other exploits. However, they are certainly not immune to any of the above; therefore, the basic principles of computer and network security apply to these computers as well. Additionally, most of the software discussed and reviewed in this book has an appropriate Macintosh version of the product.

How This Book is Organized

This book is organized to help you achieve your goals of protecting your computer or network system. It will arm you with the knowledge and tools to successfully protect your computer and network systems. Protection of your data must be a priority of any home or business user. Imagine coming home and discovering your computer has been stolen. Do you have a backup of the data? Can you restore it? How much time, money, and effort would be lost restoring the damage from the loss of a computer or network. Having your computer suffer an online attack is not much different than having your computer stolen; the loss of data might be catastrophic. The Internet is teaming with viruses, spyware, spam, and other exploitative programs designed to access your personally identifiable information; damage your business; cost you time, money, and materials; and destroy priceless family photographs stored on hard drives. Imagine losing your entire digital photograph or digital music collection. After reading this book and applying the principles and techniques contained within, you will be secure and protected from a wide range of threats.

I designed this book for the individual or small business that does not have an information technology staff or large budget. You do not need to be a computer science major to understand and apply the principles from this book. This book can potentially save you and your business countless hours of lost time and thousands of dollars in lost revenue, not to mention the mental anguish of recovering from a devastating attack on your computers or network.

I hope you find this book serves as a guide that you can reference often in the ongoing battle to protect your computers and networks from malicious and potentially devastating attacks.

CHAPTER 1

Malware:
A Comprehensive Introduction

Those who own a computer and are connected to the Internet are at risk of a malicious malware attack, hacking attempt, spam, phishing, viruses, worms, and a variety of other methods aimed at breaking into their computer or network to cause damage, steal or destroy data, or take control over their computer. People connect to the Internet to do most tasks, including e-mailing, surfing Web sites, maintaining Web sites, managing e-commerce applications, making online purchases, engaging in social networking, and more. Billions of people surf the Internet every day. Unfortunately, there are a growing number of threats they encounter each day in cyberspace.

Malware is simply malicious software and is a generic term to describe any of the wide variety of software applications designed to damage computers, servers, or networks. Typically, malware is considered to be viruses, spam, spyware, and adware, but there are many other forms of malware. One important fact to remember is that this activity is illegal. In 1996, the Computer Crime &

Intellectual Property Section, charged with enforcing cyber crime laws, became a part of the U.S. Department of Justice. The section is responsible for implementing strategies in combating computer and intellectual property crimes worldwide. The computer crime initiative is a comprehensive program designed to combat electronic penetrations, data thefts, and cyber attacks on critical information systems. The section prevents, investigates, and prosecutes computer crimes by working with other government agencies, the private sector, academic institutions, and foreign counterparts. All cyber crimes should be reported to authorities. The U.S. Department of Justice offers a guide for victims on how to report cyber crime and who they should report it to at **www.justice.gov/criminal/cybercrime/reporting.htm.**

Any time users are asked to make changes to their browser settings, change their home page, add tool bars, add plug-ins, open e-mail attachments, click on hyperlinks, download software, install software, or respond to questionable looking e-mails, they put their computers at significant risk. One might ask what exactly a person can do safely on the Internet, because many users perform these activities every day on a variety of Web sites. This is not meant to scare; most of the previously mentioned actions are safe, and with some planning and defensive tactics, users can be prepared to face most challenges and threats on the Internet.

An August 2009 report by IBM stated there was a "508 percent increase in the number of malicious Web links" that has created "an unprecedented state of Web insecurity." The X-Force 2009 Mid-Year Trend and Risk Report reported that "security threats to Web surfers are no longer limited to malicious domains or untrusted Web sites" and now include dangerous content on legitimate Internet sites. There is clearly no such thing as "safe" Web browsing any longer, as the threat of malware has grown exponentially as Internet use continues to escalate. The report paints a bleak picture for Web surfers, who now face challenges of malicious content posted on popular blogs, search engines, and Web sites. IBM reported that "Trojans accounted for 55 percent of all new malware, a 9 percent increase from the first half of 2008." Do not worry; although the threat is real, there is good news. Phishing attacks have decreased significantly in the past year, and though the number of hoaxes has not fallen significantly, the effectiveness of these hoax attempts has been greatly reduced, thanks primarily to the education of Internet users. Software manufacturers are producing products that are more capable of combating the threat of persistent and damaging malware and the availability of affordable protection has significantly increased. Operating systems, such as Microsoft Windows 7, are significantly more secure than previous versions of operating systems.

Some information and data must be passed between the browser and Web servers. Cookies, for example, have been the labeled as malware or adware for years; however, they are simply passive data files that identify and track a user's activities online. The use of cookies is how Web sites recognize someone as a returning customer and can "recommend" products of interest to them based on your shopping and browsing history. Cookies are typically very safe and improve the online experience. *This book will discuss cookies more in Chapter 6.*

This chapter will give an introduction to some of the malware threats Internet users face. This chapter will discuss each in detail and provide readers with the knowledge, tools, and skills to deter, detect, and prevent malware from affecting their computers and network systems.

Malware is typically categorized by the "damage potential" it can inflict. It is usually rated as high, medium, or low based on the capability to damage to your computer system or network. Damage is also classified as direct or indirect. Direct occurs when data is destroyed, altered, or deleted. Indirect might be bulk e-mail attacks on mail servers or denial of service attacks on Web servers, which might not cause physical damage to the hardware operating system, but can overload the capacity of the servers and disrupt functionality, often crippling business and government networks. Here is a brief, general checklist of malware categories and potential impacts:

High threat
- System instability/crashes/blue screens
- System data loss or destruction
- Network traffic overloads the server
- System recovery required
- Restoration of data from external backup
- Data exploitation (stolen data)
- Backdoor access to systems

Medium threat
- Disabling/deleting system security software (firewall, antivirus)
- Minor data modification (insertion of infections)
- System might be restored or cleaned with commercial tools
- Malware that is nondestructive on computer

- Network traffic affect servers but does not overload them
- Malware that executes nondestructive, but unknown applications

Low threat
- No obvious changes to system stability
- No obvious changes to system files
- Minor deletion of noncritical data or operating system files
- Changes to browser or system settings that can be undone by user
- Most damage is reversed with system restart

Spyware

Spyware is defined as anything that resides on a computer and can track, report, and monitor a user's activities (both online and off). Spyware is typically nonintrusive, meaning computer users most likely do not even know it is there, unless they search for it. Spyware is designed to capture information about Internet users and their activities and report it to someone else. This data might include passwords, financial data, online activity, and keystrokes. Spyware can infect a computer through Web sites, blogs, software installations, e-mails, viruses, and other delivery methods. This book dedicates an entire chapter to spyware: how to combat it, how to remove it, and how to prevent it. *See Chapter 5 for more information about this topic.*

Adware

Adware is the polar opposite of spyware. While spyware does its damage in secret, adware is typically very obvious and can be both intrusive and difficult to eradicate. Adware is software that forces banner advertisements and other forms of advertisements to appear onto a user's desktop, browser window, and more. Typically, adware appears in a Web browser and is both annoying and persistent. Despite common misconception, not all adware is installed maliciously; in fact, most adware is installed as part of another software installation. These adware installations are forced to reduce software development costs by selling advertisements. Ever bought a new computer? They are typically loaded with adware for third-party software and hardware solutions. The first thing a user should do after purchasing a new computer is reinstall a clean copy of the operating system, or at a minimum, remove all adware before connecting it to the network.

Why is adware considered to be malware when most adware will not cause damage to a computer (other than steal system resources to run)? In recent years, adware has become more offensive, often displaying pornographic or other offensive material. Another component of adware is pop-up windows. More widely used in past years, these are windows that automatically open when an Internet user visits a Web site. Often, they cannot be closed and can spawn an endless series of other pop-up windows. The good news is most modern browsers have built in pop-up blockers to prevent the windows from even opening. *Methods to remove and block adware will be included in Chapter 5.*

Viruses

A virus is malicious software designed to destroy or damage data files, operating systems, and more, and it is designed to replicate itself and spread throughout the Internet. For a virus to be effective, it must spread quickly. The faster a virus spreads and the more malicious the resulting damage, the more successful the virus is. Viruses are primarily spread through e-mail; however, they can be transmitted on discs or flash drives and reside on hard drives or in other forms of data files. Viruses can be attached to nonmalicious e-mails, meaning the sender of the e-mail likely has no idea that a virus is attached to the e-mail. Viruses can be like time bombs — some are active upon receipt, while others lie in a dormant state for hours, days, weeks, months, or even years before activating and wreaking havoc. Damage from viruses is wide-ranging — from destroying data files, deleting data, deleting critical files in the operating system, reformatting a hard drive, and even replicating through an e-mail program without a user's knowledge. Viruses are executable files — files that typically end with a .exe extension and when clicked, execute and run a program that launches a software program — that must be triggered to run; most commonly, this is through at attachment to an e-mail that a recipient must open to activate. The virus is often disguised as something else, such as an image or .HTML file. An HTML file, or HyperText Markup Language, is the primary language for Web pages. HTML is a markup language used to format Web pages for display in a Web browser, such as Internet Explorer. When the recipient opens the file, it activates the virus and it runs, attempting to replicate and execute the damage it was programmed to deliver. The good news is there are plenty of readily available defenses against viruses.

Spam

Some might question the addition of spam into the "malware" category. After all, it is mostly harmless; although, it is the primary delivery method for viruses, worms, and Trojans. Spam is simply unsolicited e-mail. It is very hard to stop, despite the use of antispam tools. Spam is much more than annoying and useless e-mails; it is illegal under federal law. Spam amounts to thousands of hours of wasted production each day across the United States as e-mail inboxes are flooded with a relentless stream of e-mails. *This book contains more information dedicated to spam, including how to combat it and how to prevent it in Chapter 4.*

Spoofing

Spoofing is done primarily in the form of e-mail spoofing; although, there are other variations, such as IP spoofing. E-mail spoofing occurs when a person receives an e-mail that appears to have come from a particular source (usually a trusted source), when it actually came from a different source. E-mail spoofing is very common with bulk e-mail or bulk-spamming. Typically, spoofing is done because the "spoofed" sender might have credibility (the user trusts that individual), so the e-mail recipient might be willing to release to them information he or she would otherwise not give out through e-mail, such as passwords or other personally identifiable information. The most common form of spoofing is receiving an e-mail that appears to come from a trusted source, such as PayPal or eBay, when in fact it has not.

E-mail spoofing is often considered the same as phishing; however, a spoofed e-mail address typically appears to have been sent by the actual proper e-mail address and SMTP server, while phishing typically uses an e-mail address similar to the proper domain, but not exactly the same (for example, support@paypal. com versus support@paypa.ru). Spoofed e-mail addresses may also appear as very long e-mail addresses, such as jduwhaush-a2u2i2214e7@verizon.net. Often, spoof and phishing e-mails ask the recipient to change his or her password for a variety of reasons, or to log into an account to verify reported fraudulent activity. The Web site the recipient is directed to is not the trusted Web site, however, and the user's data is stolen for malicious purposes, such as credit card fraud. Today, most Web mail servers restrict relaying — using a mail server to spread spam unbeknownst to the server owner — and require authentication to prevent spoofing. However, spoofing is still widespread due to the number of mail servers whose only purpose is to spread spam and spoofing e-mails.

IP spoofing allows attackers to hide their true identity on the Internet by disguising their Internet protocol address. An Internet protocol, or IP, address is a numerical identifier that is assigned to each network device in a computer network. Each computer on the Internet has an IP address, and every Web site has an IP address, which is translated into the domain name. For example, you can navigate to Amazon.com's Web site (**www.amazon.com**) in your Web browser, or you can also navigate to that site by just entering the IP address where the site is hosted, which in this case is http://72.21.207.65/. IP spoofing lets the attacker gain access to a computer by making it appear to send messages and communication from a trusted host or IP address, when in fact it is not.

In most cases, IP spoofing is used in denial of service attacks. In a denial of service attack the Web server is flooded with as many packets of data as possible within a short time span. The intent is to flood the network with heavy traffic to disrupt normal network traffic and communications. Denial of service attacks are common and difficult to defend against. These attacks can cripple network communications, effectively disabling entire entities such as government agencies or large corporations.

Phishing

Phishing is essentially the same thing as e-mail spoofing; however, phishing is targeted to "fish" for information, typically passwords, credit card numbers, or social security numbers. Many major companies have been victims of phishing. The main difference between typical e-mail spoofing and phishing is that the Web sites to which victims are directed in phishing campaigns look like the legitimate Web sites. The idea is simply to trick a computer user into thinking the e-mail and Web site are real and coax him or her into logging in, giving away his or her user name and password information.

Worms

Worms are a close cousin to viruses; the main difference is that a worm can run itself and is can replicate without any human interaction. A virus needs a host to run, while a worm runs as part of the host program. Worms typically replicate through vulnerabilities in software, operating systems, or browsers to spread across the Internet. They are also often spread through e-mail attachments, instant messenger applications, and peer-to-peer applications such as LimeWire and Kazaa.

Trojans

Trojans, also known as Trojan horses, are named after the famous Trojan horse used in the fall of the city of Troy. Trojans are files or applications that users allows to be installed on their computer, believing them to be beneficial or not harmful. Peer-to-peer networks and music sharing Web sites are common sources for

Trojans. A user downloads a file, believing it to be a benign MP3 file. After launching the file, the user discovers that it is not an MP3 file; it is a destructive Trojan that is now installed on his or her system. Trojans are very destructive and can be created to destroy data, reformat hard drives, delete data, or alter operating systems. Trojans often install hidden applications, such as keystroke loggers, which capture keyboard activity and ultimately reveal passwords, credit card numbers, social security numbers, and sensitive information to others.

SQL Injection

Structured query language (SQL) is used to store and retrieve data from a database using a set of standard query commands. SQL is used throughout the Web on database-driven Web sites. These happen on a site that asks users to put in variables and takes these variables and runs a command through a database, such as displaying a list of all customers with the last name "Smith." With an SQL injection, malicious code is put into the variable, so when the database performs the task, it will follow the malicious code's instructions. This could manipulate or delete data

SQL injection is unique from other forms of attack because the attacker is actually exploiting vulnerabilities in the Web site coding and using those vulnerabilities to inflict damage, instead of installing a virus or executing software from a third-party. SQL injection is complex and the primary defense — unlike other forms of malware — lies in how a Web page that uses an SQL server, or other SQL-based databases, is built.

Hijack

Hijacking can take many forms. Hijacking is a type of attack in which the communications and control of a computer system or network is taken over and controlled by another entity. Hijacked communications might allow access to users' communications and network data packets, enabling the nefarious parties to modify or replace that information with other information. Data is transmitted and travels through the Internet in network data packets. For example, the network breaks apart an e-mail message into multiple parts called packets. Each of these packets contains some of the original information in the e-mail and carries identifying information to ensure that it gets to the proper destination — the sender's IP address. Upon receipt, these packets are reassembled so the receiver can read the complete e-mail. In some forms of hijacking, another party assumes control of a computer or network, preventing the user from having any control over his or her systems.

A more common form of hijacking is Web browser hijacking, in which another party assumes control over a Web browser and the user is directed to a different Web site from the one to which he or she intended to navigate. Often, hijacked browsers spawn new browser windows when closed, making it difficult to get rid of the unwanted browser sessions, and more times than not, the Web sites are offensive or pornographic in nature.

Browser hijacking can get very technical in nature. Attackers can actually alter Domain Name System (DNS) server entries by modifying them to redirect traffic to another fraudulent site. The DNS is a system to organize and identify domains. DNS provides a domain name for a domain's Internet protocol (IP) address. It would be very difficult to remember the IP address for most of the Web sites we visit; a DNS server converts this unique number into the domain name. For example, instead of remembering http://72.21.207.65/, you can simply type in Amazon.com's Web site (**www.amazon.com**) in your Web browser and both take you to the same site. Your DNS server will convert this number to the domain name automatically.

By altering the DNS entry for a domain name, site visitors are redirected to another Web page. These can be replicated version of the actual pages and used to capture personally identifiable information, credit card numbers, or passwords, or more often, they are pornographic Web sites. These attacks are highly effective because the Web site owner is likely to believe his or her site has been hacked into and modified, when in fact the Web site is perfectly fine on the Web server, but the browser has been directed by the modified DNS entry to a fake Web site on another Web server. This is also commonly known as a "spoofed" Web site.

Rootkits

Originally, rootkits were a set of tools built within the UNIX operating system, which is an open source operating system. Open source software lets users access the original source code and redistribute the code for free. The UNIX tools were modified and used to gain unauthorized access to the computer while concealing this access from system administrators. Rootkits are a major concern for Microsoft Windows-based operating systems as well. A Windows rootkit is a program that conceals files, registry entries, and memory addresses from the operating system or other running programs. Rootkits are built into an operating system (just like UNIX) to serve a specific purpose, and therefore, they are not by themselves considered malware. Malware can use rootkits to make modifications to the operating system, create unauthorized access points, and install other applications within the computer, all undetected by the user, the operating system, or potentially even security software running on the computer. For example, rootkits can be used to install and hide viruses or spyware in the computer that is undetected by the user or any antivirus applications. Again, rootkits are part of the operating system and are often used legitimately to protect data and portions of the operating system. Rootkits are classified as persistent, meaning they activate every time the computer is started, or nonpersistent, meaning they run and do their damage, but will not run again upon a computer restart. Rootkits can cause a wide variety of damage to the infected computer; however, as with most malware, the goal is to steal data for financial gain. Yet some rootkits are aimed at destroying computer data and disrupting network operations or productivity.

Rootkits can be a persistent challenge; there are some rootkits that remain intact even after a disk reformat and operating system reinstall. Rootkits are very complicated and require *advanced knowledge* of the operating system on which they are installed. *The Rootkit Arsenal: Escape and Evasion in the Dark Corners of the System*, by Bill Blunden, is a detailed resource for learning about rootkits. Rootkits are difficult to detect and even more difficult to remove. Third-party software is available to help identify and remove malware rootkits from an operating system. *This will be discussed further in Chapter 11.*

Bots

A bot is defined as an infected computer that has illicit software installed on it. This software allows another, remote computer to control it. As with most malware, software is installed maliciously without the knowledge of the computer user. Often bots are installed unintentionally as part of another software installation and are widely distributed through e-mail, peer-to-peer networks, and instant messenger applications. Botnets are a collection of similarly infected computers controlled by other computers in a collaborated effort. In most cases, the intent of a botnet is to use a computer (or many computers composing the botnet) as relays for spam, for denial of service attacks, and to attack other computers or networks.

Bots range widely in characteristics and purpose and are often difficult to detect. One of the best ways to detect a bot is to monitor network traffic reports, which detect unusually high activity when a bot is installed on a system. Bots are often undetectable to even the latest versions of spyware detection software. In many cases, the only way to remove a bot is to reformat the hard drive and reinstall the operating system. Often, bots are hidden by rootkits, making them undetectable to many disinfectant programs. Bots are self-replicating in nature, and they frequently spread themselves as URLs (Web addresses) embedded in e-mails or instant messenger applications through contact and buddy lists. If recipients click on the links because they trust the sender of the e-mail or instant message, they become infected, and the process repeats on the recipients' systems.

Bots are a very real, growing threat. They are increasingly harder to detect and remove from infected systems. As mentioned earlier, rootkits are commonly used to hide bots, increasing the difficulty of detection and inoculation. The Federal Bureau of Investigation (FBI) coined the term "bot-herder" for "hackers who install malicious software on computers through the Internet without the owners' knowledge. Once the software is loaded, they can control the computer remotely. And once they have compromised enough computers, they have a robot network or botnet."

The FBI reported that some botnets consist of tens of thousands of infected computers. The FBI has an ongoing operation called "Operation Bot Roast," which is a coordinated initiative to disrupt and dismantle botnets. The FBI also charged many individuals with cyber crimes, including using botnets to send tens of millions of spam messages, infecting tens of thousands of computers worldwide, and using botnets to disable other systems.

Impact of Malware

Malware can have a tremendous, negative impact on home and business computers and networks. It can dramatically reduce the performance of a computer system; destroy data and operating systems; force hardware failures; delete critical files; modify files; cause system crashes; expose personally identifiable information, credit card numbers, financial records, and social security numbers; compromise computer and network security settings; enable bulk spam e-mails; and more.

The best defense against malware is a strong offense. This book will detail each step to protecting a system from malware, but it is important to pay attention to a computer, where often signs of potential infection, spyware, adware, and malware will appear. Symptoms such as an extremely busy hard drive when no other activity is running, e-mails a user never sent that bounce back to him or her, and changes in browser settings that the user did not originate are all indications of potential problems. Changes in browser settings include the set home page or how a pop-up blocker works. New shortcuts, folders, and files that a user does not recognize and did not install might be potentially damaging files.

Avoid peer-to-peer sharing sites. Do not use any illegal file sharing software or share and exchange illegal files over the Internet. Some peer to peer or file sharing software is used for the distribution of very large files, popular files, and files available for free; however, it is also used to illegally download copyrighted software, music, and movies.

Computer users should be very careful of which banner advertising they click on while surfing the Web, especially on unfamiliar Web sites. Banner ads will take Internet surfers to third-party sites, whose trustworthiness is unknown. Surfers should be careful of what links they click on, even those from "trusted" sites. Researchers at Kaspersky Labs estimate one in every 500 Web site addresses in Twitter posts point to sites hosting malware. Twitter, a social networking site, lets users post tweets that are 140 characters or less. To meet this character limit, many users post shortened versions of Web addresses as links to some topic they want to share. The compression of URLs in Twitter posts helps hide the real URL and helps spread malware. Twitter, recognizing the problem, has initiated a filtering system to detect and remove malicious URLs or warns users before they click on the URL.

So how can Internet surfers protect themselves and tell if a Web site is safe to visit or not? Both Google and Microsoft offer tools to help with this endeavor. Google Safe Browsing diagnostics offers a simple way to check the safety of any Web site. Internet users can visit the Google URL **www.google.com/safebrowsing/diagnostic?site=http://www.yoursite.com**, and replace "yoursite.com" with the domain name they want to review. They will get a detailed report as shown in the following figure:

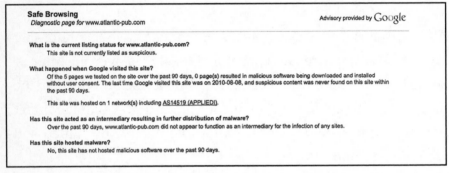

Google Screenshots™ Used with Permission from Google, Inc.

As the resource shows, Atlantic Publishing Group Inc.'s Web site is perfectly safe. Here is another Web site that appears to be a site that might host malware:

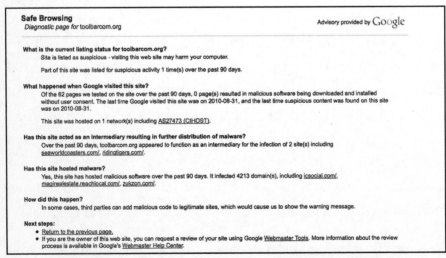

Google Screenshots™ Used with Permission from Google, Inc.

Microsoft Bing, which replaced Microsoft Live Search, also has malware detection tools in its search engine. These tools automatically filter out sites that have malware detected on them in the search results.

This book will delve into malware and many other threat topics, but here is a handy resource guide of Web sites with the most current and relevant data on malware protection and the very latest threat assessments:

- Computer Emergency Response Team (CERT) (**www.cert. org**): Addresses risks at the software and system level.

- Symantec (**www.symantec.com/security_response**): Provides customers with comprehensive, global, 24/7 Internet security expertise to guard against today's complex Internet threats.

- McAfee (**www.mcafee.com/us/threat_center/default.asp**): A source for the latest global threat intelligence, assessments, and tools.

- Microsoft (**www.microsoft.com/security**): The security center for all Microsoft products.

- TrendMicro (**http://threatinfo.trendmicro.com**): Includes an updated threat encyclopedia including spyware, malware, and viruses.

- Vupen (**www.vupen.com/english/malware-advisories**): Includes updated security malware advisories.

- Microsoft Malware Protection Site (**www.microsoft.com/ security/portal**): Provides world-class antimalware research and response capabilities that support Microsoft's range of security products and services.

Symantec Corp. states the "worst is yet to come." In its 2010 Security Predictions report, available at **www.symantec.com/connect/ blogs/worst-yet-come-symantec-s-2010-security-predictions**, Symantec reports on a variety of growing threats to Internet, computers, and network security. Sunbelt Software, a Clearwater, Florida-based provider of endpoint and server-based security software for the enterprise, consumer, and original equipment manufacturer (OEM) markets states that "malware infection rates (are) on the rise" and "the rate at which legitimate Web sites have been infected with malicious code has risen sharply in recent months, to 640,000 infected Web sites and 5.8 million pages." The full report can be read by visiting Sunbelt Software's Web site at **www.sunbeltsoftware.com/About/Security-News**.

This book will discuss tools available to combat malware, as well as provide Internet surfers with the essential information to protect their systems from intrusion; however, one of the most common ways to protect oneself is to ensure Web browsers and operating systems routinely receive patches and upgrades. Microsoft and Apple make this very simple: Computer users can schedule updates to download and install without any intervention, so there is no reason an operating system should not updated. Despite this easy system, a large percentage of computers are not routinely updated and are running with known exposures to potential malware attacks.

CHAPTER 2

Computer Viruses: Are You at Risk?

This chapter is designed to provide a brief introduction to viruses, symptoms of viruses, and the variety of threats Internet surfers face on today. Viruses are a real threat, even with antivirus software, due to the nature of recently created viruses. As good as most antivirus manufacturers are, they are a step behind virus developers. Antivirus manufacturers create signatures to detect and remove viruses that are already circulating through the Internet.

Following safe security practices and using modern, updated antivirus, antimalware, and antispyware programs in combination with a strong personal firewall and common sense will protect most users from today's threats on the Internet. This book will dig deep into each topic area and ensure users are well-educated and well-prepared for the onslaught of threats they will face on the Internet as they protect their home or business computers and networks.

A computer virus can be any piece of program developed by a hacker or software programmer whose sole purpose is to make the infected computer system malfunction or to destroy data on the infected computer. Virus programmers try to disguise the virus program as some ordinary, often-used type of file or a file that users will be tempted to open. A virus program is typically an executable file (for example, casino.exe), but a virus program can be embedded or coded into any binary file — a computer file that may contain data — encoded in binary form for computer storage and processing purposes, typically noticeable by a .bin file extension, including pictures and movies.

Antivirus programs often detect common viruses. Some hackers are able to design the pattern of a virus in such a stealthy and modernized manner that it can easily bypass the antivirus program and infect the computer system. The reason these programs are named after the medical term "virus" is that they work in a similar manner: replicating themselves into every other possible executable file and damaging both computer systems and users' important data to the greatest extent possible. Also like a biological virus, computer viruses are contagious and strong. They affect not only the system from which the virus was first executed, but can affect other computer systems as well by any means of communication. Viruses can transfer to other computers through file or print network sharing, an infected virus program on a USB device, or e-mail.

Computer viruses first came to notice in the public when the use of computer systems became popular in the 1980s. As more people learned the art of computer science, more people started to gain expertise in this specialized field. The term "hacker" became famous as malicious computer engineers and software developers started to create programs and techniques that could compromise remote computer systems (any random or targeted computer system online) and either destroy their data or gain access to their private and confidential data. Apart from doing this online, a hacker could program a virus and either distribute it via any media format — including floppy disk, CD, and USB flash drive — all with the intent of the virus spreading from one computer to another, infecting each as it goes. These offline viruses do not necessarily let the computer hackers gain access to the infected computer, but they can severely damage and cripple the affected computer system by deleting data or harming other features of the operating system.

A program developed to compromise computer systems via the Internet is called a "Trojan horse," which usually does not damage the operating system, whereas a program that can also damage or destroy the computer operating system is called a "virus." There is another way of compromising and gaining access to a remote computer system online. Programs can exploit the operating system or a specific service running on the remote computer system by exploiting possible vulnerabilities on it and using those vulnerabilities for remote access, theft of data, and more. Because widespread use of the Internet came much later than the use of computers themselves, the development and popularity of computer viruses is considered older than the development of Trojan horses and other computer exploitation tools.

Why are there viruses and why were viruses developed in the first place? It is the same reason there are thieves in the world, the same reason there are bullies, the same reason individuals or groups of individuals inflict harm upon others. It really comes down to the basic psychology of a person who uses his or her talents to create malicious computer viruses.

There are many reasons why someone might create a virus or malware. In some cases, it is simply to test his or her programming skills and to see if he or she can create a virus and then watch how potent the virus is once it is released or how quickly it spreads. Some people might create viruses for fame or to create a name for themselves as the "creator" of a popular virus. Often, viruses and/or malware are created for revenge against individuals, corporations, or government agencies for some perceived prosecution or maltreatment. Other reasons can be as simple as to generate business for selling software to "clean" or "remove" the virus or to generate fear in the minds of the computer user. People also create viruses and malware to steal personal information, perpetuate identify theft, or access financial data. The reasons for creating viruses and malware are endless and varied, and understanding the reasons behind the creative motivation for developing and releasing viruses and malware is often elusive and might never be understood.

Types of Viruses

A virus can be more than just an attractive-looking file or ordinary file that we often use. Viruses can be categorized into a few types, as explained below:

Program file viruses

Also known as binary file viruses, program file viruses are the most common, because they are easier to program than other. Such viruses are found in executable files whose file name extension can be .exe, .com, .bat, and .scr. A file name extension is a suffix appended to the name of a computer file and is typically used to define what type of file it is. They can also be in other binary and system files — such as .bin, .olv, .drv, .sys, and .ocx — and image and movie files — such as JPEGs, GIFs, AVI, and MPEG. Some examples of program file viruses are: Virus.Win32.Sality.aa, Packed.Win32.Krap.b, and Packed.Win32.Black.a.

Macro viruses

A macro virus is usually programmed to damage a computer user's database, which is a collection of data. This type of virus is found in office applications such as Microsoft Excel, Microsoft Word, and Adobe Flash. A macro virus is as dangerous and devastating as other types of viruses. Some examples of these are Melissa virus, DMV, Nuclear, and Concept.

Boot sector viruses

Boot sector viruses are complicated to design but they are the most dangerous and devastating viruses of all. In computers, booting refers to the process that starts an operating system, like Microsoft Windows. This virus attacks either the boot sector of the media — including the hard disk, floppy disk, and USB flash drive — or it can also infect the master boot record, which is where the computer BIOS — the basic input/output system of a computer — looks to load the initial boot program, which begins the processing of loading and launching the operating system. Thus, this type of virus is hard or, in some cases, impossible to remove, rendering a computer completely nonfunctional. Some examples of boot sector viruses are Disk Killer, Michelangelo, and the Stone virus.

Logic bombs

As the name suggests, logic bomb viruses are highly intelligent and logical in function, as they are only triggered upon specific tasks, scenarios, and conditions. An example would be arrival on a specific date or execution when a user performs a specific task such as launching Internet Explorer or updating Windows. A logic bomb contains malicious code that may stay hidden or inert until meeting specific conditions, which would then trigger activation. A logic bomb is typically triggered by an event, such as printing a document or a virus that waits to execute until it has infected a certain number of hosts. However, a time bomb, which is a subset of the logic bomb, is set to activate by a specific date or time. The most famous time bomb is the Friday the 13th virus, which infects two other files upon execution of the original file, and on the date of Friday the 13th, the virus will delete any infected file as it is executed.

Companion viruses

Although companion viruses are obsolete, they are still found in rare conditions. Companion viruses affect only the MS-DOS environment, which is the predecessor operating environment to Windows XP, Vista, and Windows 7. MS-DOS was still built into the operating system shell for Windows 3.x and Microsoft Windows Millenium Edition (Me). Because MS-DOS is less used these days, encountering companion viruses is becoming very infrequent. This type of virus affects core MS-DOS-based files, such as .com files and .exe files. If this virus affects COMMAND. COM — the default filename of the operating system shell for DOS operating systems, and command line on 16/32-bit versions of Windows 9x/Me — the damage can cause an entire hard drive to malfunction or not perform at all.

Self-modifying code (viruses)

More logical and sophisticated than logic bombs, self-modifying viruses are programmed to modify themselves. This type of virus keeps changing its pattern internally so it can evade the filtering system of antivirus software and infect systems. An example of this type of virus is the Win95.Zmist.A virus.

Network virus

Also known as a computer worm, a network virus not only replicates itself via networks — a collection of computers and devices connected by wired or wireless communications — to other computer systems, but also affects the infected computer by leeching the network bandwidth — the amount of data passing through a connection — and making the user's Internet and network connection quite slow. An example of this type of virus is Email-Worm.Win32.Merond.a.

E-mail virus

An e-mail virus, which is delivered and transmitted via e-mails, has the ability to shake the foundations of some of the biggest technology companies. When programmed intelligently, these viruses not only can cause unimaginable damage to a computer system, but can also spread themselves from one e-mail to the e-mail addresses found in the infected recipient's contact list. Examples of this include Mydoom, the Melissa virus, and the ILOVEYOU virus.

Multipartite viruses

Multipartite viruses can affect computers in more than one way. They are capable of infecting both program files and boot sectors of a hard disk and are a very dangerous type of virus. Once executed while the computer is running, it writes to boot sectors, damaging both the working environment and boot sectors. Examples of multipartite viruses include Tequila and Invader.

Script-based viruses

Apart from being a binary file, a virus can be in a simple script file, which contains a series of commands that are processed in order when executed. A simple script file can also be a batch file — a file that contains a series of commands that are executed in order when the batch file is run — typically ending in .bat and normally found in a Unix or MS-DOS operating environment. Batch files can be executed even in Windows XP's command prompt — the command line interpreter in Windows Operating Systems — and Linux's shell environment, the Linux's command line interface. It can also be a JavaScript or Visual Basic script file, a script that is executed when loaded by a Web browser.

Although the items in the following list are not viruses by their nature and pattern, they were initially inspired by the concept of a virus and can be included as miscellaneous types of viruses.

Trojan horse

The working of a Trojan horse is similar to that of its namesake. It disguises itself as a surprise file that appears legitimate (for example, the file the user wanted to use), but in reality it will invade a system and let a hacker gain access to the infected computer system. Because almost all antivirus software can detect and eliminate viruses and Trojan horses, these programs are becoming more obsolete every day.

Spyware

The purpose of spyware is to collect information about the victim and send that information back to the team or person who developed the spyware. Spyware is covered in significant detail throughout this book and can take on a variety of forms.

Keyloggers

Keyloggers are a limited form of spyware, because they are programmed only to record keystrokes of the computer user and send them back to a hacker. Keyloggers can be used to record passwords and other confidential data, which the program sends back to the hacker as a log file that can be read to compromise user names, passwords, financial data, and other personally identifiable information.

How Viruses Infect Computers

The working mechanics of a virus depend on the type of virus it is. As described earlier, each type of virus infects the computer in its own unique way, but all viruses have the same purpose: to destroy or damage the computer system and/or data. If a virus is not a boot sector virus, then it commonly resides in the memory and affects targeted files, either when they are executed by the computer user or by just exploring the folders from the Windows Explorer (for example, My Computer).

There are typically two patterns in which a virus infects computer files. One way is to infect the computer files completely, so an antivirus program cannot clean the virus. The other way is to just infect a portion of the files, thus allowing antivirus software to clean and remove the infection. It all depends on the creativity of the virus programmer and the advancement of the antivirus program used. There are some viruses that cannot be removed with antivirus software unless you have the latest virus definitions installed; thus, it is critical to ensure an antivirus application is updated with new virus signatures daily. Viruses also affect computer files by resizing them, deleting them permanently, randomly corrupting them, or crashing the computer system.

Sometimes, upon execution, a virus makes its variants and alias — altered forms of the virus that are hidden in other places on the computer not normally looked at or disguised as legitimate files — in folders that a normal computer user will not look at. They can make themselves invisible and undetectable while antivirus software is either randomly or specifically scanning for them. This pattern of viruses makes them more dangerous and stealthy in nature, causing significant and devastating damage to the computer operating system and user files. The ideal goal of a virus is to infect a computer system without a user's permission and without letting the user know the system is infected. A user often will not know they are infected until the antivirus software detects the virus or the user realizes the computer system is damaged or data is destroyed. This is why computer users should ensure they have a solid backup program to protect their data in case of a devastating loss of integrity.

Capabilities of a Virus

A virus's severity and security risk is measured by its capability. For instance, a virus can be as harmless as a program that creates several folders in a hard drive, just to consume disk space.

Virus creators might make these viruses to taunt the victims, test the response of antivirus software manufacturers, or cause havoc without creating any "real" permanent damage. A user can undo the damage by deleting those files. A malicious virus, however, can cause significantly more damage by deleting data from the computer or corrupting information. A well-designed and pro-grammed virus can significantly damage not only the operations system and data files, but also the hardware of the computer system. Remember, a virus's goal is to damage the computer system and/or data by hiding itself, replicating, and being undetectable and unstoppable. For instance, if a virus is to hide itself from a common computer user, it can pretend to be an ordinary system or data file that a user will be likely to open or execute. When a virus is programmed to hide itself from an antivirus, it can cam-ouflage itself in the system files of the user, either by hiding in core system folders as a phony system file or by being resident in the memory, as an altered system file that has been modified by a virus.

Some viruses can prevent computer systems from performing se-curity measurements that could reveal the virus's presence. For instance, a virus can prevent a computer user from performing the "Ctrl+Alt+Del" function to launch the task manager, which shows all processes currently running in system memory, so the user cannot see that a suspicious file or service is resident in the memory. Viruses can stop the computer and sometimes antivirus software from performing certain security tasks. Furthermore, apart from residing in memory as fake system files, viruses can also inject code in core system files, thus corrupting the core func-tioning of the computer's operating system. An antivirus, if un-able to clean the virus, cannot undo the damage done to core system files, resulting in permanent damage to the operating system and requiring a system restore, repair, or clean installation.

The following are some practical explanations of the capabilities and symptoms of computer viruses:

- It can slow down the computer. Users will feel a great difference in speed if their computers are infected; however, a slower computer might refer to some other issues, including congested disk space or too many programs opened at the same time.

- It can cause the computer to frequently hang/stick (stop responding) or crash, especially when executing a program, such as messenger software or Internet Explorer.

- It can make a computer restart unexpectedly without user's interaction or other indication.

- It can cause frequently used computer applications to suddenly start working "weird" or no longer function.

- It can tamper with the system's security levels and read and write levels of a hard drive, thus making the user unable to access the hard drive or providing delete privileges to protected file areas. In doing so, it can prevent you from removing infected files and can permanently delete critical, protected system files.

- It can fill up the disk space, making the performance of the hard disk poor and preventing the user from installing or writing anything to the hard disk.

- It can rename files and folders to deceive the computer user.

- In some cases it can deactivate or disable the antivirus program the computer user has, making the virus more progressive and unstoppable.

- It is capable of launching pop-ups and play sounds, movie files, etc. Virus-launched pop-ups often contain sexually explicit text or images.

- It is capable of shutting down a running computer program abruptly without the user's interaction or permission.

A network virus can open ports in a computer system and send malicious packets to remote computers over the network, thereby slowing the network down or causing the entire network to become congested with traffic.

Locations Where a Virus is Most Commonly Found

Viruses are most commonly found on:

- **Music CDs, DVDs, and video game discs**. In countries where pirated CDs, DVDs, or video games discs are often sold, the chances of viruses being included are drastically increased;

- **Pornographic Web sites**. Apart from paid pornographic Web sites, most free pornographic sites contain viruses and malicious scripts that could harm users' computers;

- **Sites that contain information about hacking.** Usually a Web site that is meant to provide information about how to hack a computer contains viruses that infect the system of those curious to learn computer hacking skills;

- **Sites that feature illegal downloads, peer-to-peer networks, file-sharing networks, and shareware.**

Impact of Viruses on Computer Operating Systems

The operating system is the heart of a computer. The operating system, commonly referred to as the OS, is the software (Windows, Linux, or Unix, for example) that interfaces with the computer hardware and other software such as office suites, Web browsers, and more. Although the central processing unit (CPU) of the computer allows the computer to operate, the operating system feeds the CPU commands and manages all running processes, services, and other resources in the execution and operation of the computer.

Microsoft Windows

Almost every virus is designed for the Microsoft Windows environment because Microsoft Windows is a closed-source application, which is a program whose source code a computer user cannot modify on his or her own according to the user's needs and desires. Furthermore, it is easier to develop a virus for a Microsoft Windows platform as compared to other operating systems because of how the code is written for programs using Windows. Previous versions of Microsoft Windows had significant exploits and weaknesses that were targeted by hackers and others with malicious intent. Fortunately, Microsoft releases security patches quickly and frequently. With the passage of time, Microsoft has worked hard to overcome vulnerabilities and security holes. In fact, Windows 7 is the most secure version of Windows yet produced. Besides earlier versions' vulnerabilities, viruses commonly exist in Windows because Microsoft Windows is the most widely used operating system in the world; hence hackers usually spend more time making viruses for this environment because this is the operating system they are using.

Linux

Because Linux is usually used by savvy computer users a environment is open source, meaning people can compile compile and build or rebuild applications easily, the popularity of viruses in Linux environments is quite limited in comparison to Windows. There are still viruses for the Linux system, though most well-equipped Linux users can tackle them quite easily even without the need of installing any antivirus programs. Unlike Windows, Linux is not as popular nor as widely used, so many hackers do not spend their time writing viruses for Linux.

Also, it is somewhat more difficult to code a virus for Linux in comparison to Windows. Although projects, such as Ubuntu Linux, are delivering Linux CDs for free worldwide and the use of Linux has grown in popularity due to free distribution and highly customizable, open-source code, Windows and Macintosh operating systems are overwhelming in comparison, and there is no significant market for Linux-based viruses.

Macintosh

Even though the Macintosh operating system is used widely among businesses and is very popular in the public environment, the popularity of writing computer viruses to affect Macintosh computers is minimal. Regardless, Mac users must take security precautions to ensure they are adequately protected.

Virus Removal Methods

The removal of a virus depends on the pattern and nature of the virus. Some viruses are easily removed and some are much more difficult to remove. Rare types of viruses cannot be removed and might require clean installation of the operation system after formatting the hard drive. Below are some security measures that can be taken to generally remove and prevent a virus from infecting a computer system:

Registry cleaning

Sometimes a virus attempts to spread itself via the registry of the victim's PC. The registry of a computer is a database built into the operating system that stores configuration settings, software, and operating system information. A virus can add registry entries, alter registry entries, or delete critical registry entries to damage the computer or help the virus to spread throughout the memory specifically during computer startup. Therefore, keeping a registry clean of suspicious and malicious entries can help a system prevent viruses from spreading to and infecting it.

Updating the operating system

Users who have not installed the latest security updates and patches for their operating systems are exposing their computers to significant risk of infection or attack by viruses and hackers who may exploit computers whose security updates have not been installed. To prevent this from happening, it is critical users always keep their systems updated.

Antivirus software

A computer must have updated, active antivirus software running to prevent a virus from infecting it and to detect and remove viruses that have already infected a system. Both Windows and Macintosh operating systems will inform you if you do not have antivirus software installed, and they will also let you know if the software is out of date. We will cover antivirus software in depth in later chapters of this book.

Virus removal tools

These tools are designed to remove specific viruses from a system. They are typically available for free from most antivirus manufacturers' Web sites and primarily released to target specific and recently discovered viruses or viruses that are persistent and difficult to remove.

Antimalware tools

Some malware are not detected by many antivirus applications, thus requiring the computer user to use appropriate tools to handle malware. An antimalware tool is used to eliminate irritating programs that cause systems to malfunction or slow down from the system. Antimalware options are covered in depth in later chapters of this book.

Antispyware tools

As with malware, it is necessary to remove possible spyware from a system as well. Even though spyware is technically malware, the use of an antispyware application, such as Microsoft Windows Defender, which is free and included with Windows

Vista, is strongly recommended; however, you will find that any reputable malware program also combats spyware.

Online guides

Even though a common virus will be eliminated by following the above procedures, it is always handy for computer users to search the Internet for removal guides or discussion groups that can help them deal with virus removal. Furthermore, it is also good for users to read about the latest viruses so they can stay educated and on the lookout for suspicious files or signs of infection.

Dos and Don'ts for Avoiding a Computer Virus

- **Do not click on suspicious looking icons on your desktop, especially if it says something about casinos or sex/porn or is some other unidentified file. If it is a shortcut, be sure to right-click on it and check its location by looking at the file.**

- **Do not open a USB/pen drive directly by double clicking it. Always open it by typing its drive letter (for example, G:\) in the address bar to help prevent accidental launch of infected files.**

- **Always scan flash drives and external drives with antivirus software before opening them to ensure they are virus free, using your antivirus software.**

- **Avoid porn, pirating, and other malicious sites. This will save you from being invaded by malicious viruses and other malware. Be sure to install antivirus software and use a browser with pop-up blockers.**

- **Do open files sent to you by strangers over the Internet.**

- Some instant messengers can reveal your IP address if a hacker is trying to send you a file. Do not accept the file nor decline it; simply close your conversation window. If your IP address is revealed to a hacker, they can do any number of dangerous things to your computer. Unless the file is from a trusted source, never accept it.

- Do not accept or send Webcam or voice chat requests to a stranger.

- Do not use more than one antivirus application at a time; otherwise they both will conflict with each other, which will cause them to be ineffective.

- Do use antispyware, antimalware, or antispam applications in addition to antivirus software for full protection.

- Always keep checking whether your antivirus is updated or not and whether it is enabled or not. If your antivirus is disabled by itself without your interaction, this is an indicator of an infection on the computer.

- Install a reputable personal firewall, which is a software or hardware barrier that protects your computer against unauthorized access.

- Be sure to scan CDs and DVDs with antivirus software before installing any software or accessing any files on the discs.

- If a picture or movie file you opened causes a change in system performance or other unusual activity you likely executed a virus or malware. Run a complete system scan for viruses, spyware, and malware.

- Keep track of background processes whenever your system slows down or malfunctions and terminate any suspicious processes. Use   to help identify unknown processes running on your computer.

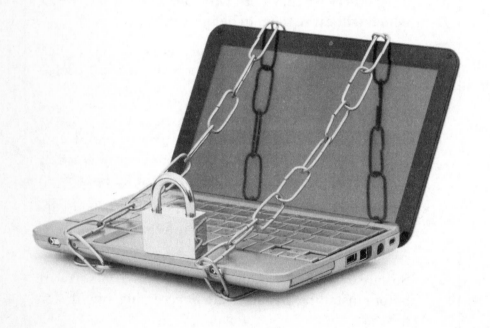

CHAPTER 3

Antivirus Solutions & Defense

Computer viruses can deliver a disastrous payload, leaving a path of destruction in their wake as they rapidly spread across the Internet. Viruses can be defeated, prevented, detected, and removed from infected systems with modern antivirus protection software that is updated routinely. When it comes to viruses and malware, it pays to be paranoid and protect a home's or business's most critical data and data networks.

Exposure risks can vary widely based on which operating system a computer runs, which e-mail program a person is using, how many individuals use a computer or network, the volume of e-mail received, the effectiveness of antispam software, and how often the antivirus software is updated. Operating systems must be patched, or corrected to fix a problem, routinely. Microsoft releases patches on the second Tuesday of the month and users should make sure their computers are set to automatically check and download updates. The effectiveness of firewalls (hardware and software) also plays directly into the exposure rating of computers and networks. User activity can also affect exposure ratings. If a user often connects to public hotspots or insecure wireless networks, accesses peer-to peer-networks, uses file sharing services, downloads files from unknown sources, or uses programs such as BitTorrent, LimeWire, Kazaa, or other services, he or she greatly increases the chance of malicious attack or infection and must take the necessary steps to secure his or her computer.

One major influence on a computer's exposure to viruses is the volume of e-mail a user receives and the quantity of that which is junk or spam e-mails. The more a person's e-mail address is proliferated throughout the Internet — the more junk mailing lists, bulk mailing lists, and illicit mailing lists he or she is on — increases the chances of receiving viruses through e-mail.

Although the use of floppy drives is nearly non-existent these days, the use of flash drives is increasing. These portable, high-capacity USB thumb drives can carry enormous amounts of information in a small package. They can be self-executing, which means they automatically launch and operate without any manual activation, when installed and deliver a dangerous payload simply by being inserted into an open USB slot. A computer user should ask himself or herself how difficult it would be for someone to put a thumb drive into a USB slot on his or her computer. Would the installed antivirus software be able to combat the threat?

Security comes as a cost, or does it? Personal firewall software, antivirus software, antimalware software, antispam software, and other security software can be obtained for free. All of this software is reputable, effective, and is updated to ensure it is armed with the latest virus definitions and patches available. By some computer experts' estimates, at least 25 percent of computers have no antivirus software installed on them. More than 50 percent have an older version (more than two versions out of date) of antivirus software and in most cases, if the computer is more than one year old, the subscription has expired and the antivirus software is ineffective against the latest threats. Products such as Microsoft Security Essentials are effective and updated often.

In Chapter 1, this book discussed signs a virus is present on a computer. Antivirus software is an application that detects malware and viruses, as well as prevents them from activating and spreading. Malware is short for "malicious software," which is any software whose goal is to harm the computer system it is on or its user, and sometimes both. A virus is a piece of software intended to delete or damage a user's files, harm computer systems, and spread itself to more computers via the infected user's computer and other means.

Antivirus software treats a wide array of malware — including Trojan horses, computer viruses, adware, spyware, and worms. How much malware it can treat depends on its version and functionality.

Older versions of antivirus software do not offer support for most malware, because such programs were not as widely known or used when the antivirus was written. Most older versions of antivirus software were designed to combat viruses only, unlike modern software that combats viruses and other malware.

Some antivirus software products search for viruses using signatures. Viruses operate in certain ways and contain certain code, and those patterns are called a signature. The signature method is limited but very effective for known viruses. Antivirus software based solely on the signature method is effective only if it is updated regularly. Antivirus software is routinely, and usually daily, updated with signatures of previous viruses. Based on these signatures, the programs check for the presence of that virus on the computer system.

The problem with the signature method is that it is ineffective against new viruses or previous viruses that were changed a bit to create a variant of the virus. The variant acts differently enough that the previous signature will not detect and destroy the virus. Here is a hypothetical example: Malicious programmers created a virus named Viru. After antivirus software creators develop ways to detect a signature based on Viru, the virus is no longer effective. Then, an attacker will change it so antivirus software with signatures to detect Viru are no longer effective and the new virus will start infecting computers. The variant will be named Viru.A. Previous experience has shown that virus writers do not give up on a virus easily and there can be as many as ten variants of one virus, with each needing a new signature entered into the antivirus program to counter it.

With the signature-based method, a user must always be alert so as to not be infected with a new virus. This means either being alert enough to update software regularly or telling it to update automatically. All modern antivirus software has automatic updates, but some programs are fee-based and will not update when your subscription expires. To get updates automatically, a user will need a working Internet connection. One common problem with signature updates is problems in downloading or installing, leaving computers unprotected against the latest threats. Using antivirus software that only uses the signature-based method of protection is the absolute bare minimum needed to protect a system.

To fix issues with the signature method of detection, some antivirus developers add generic virus signatures, which are not specific to one virus but are patterns that many viruses share. This method detects the latest virus threats, but it can also have many false positives, identifying perfectly safe files as potential viruses. Most antivirus programs allow users to automatically take certain actions against a suspected file, such as delete them. Users must be cautious to ensure they are not deleting critical system files.

Most antivirus software products also combat malware and some have built-in firewalls and other system tools that will meet most or all of users' computer security needs. These all-inclusive security suites provide users with one simple solution; however, most are fee-based for both the software and annual update service. *Many of these are discussed in Chapter 11.*

Some antivirus programs can seriously slow down a computer's speed due to using too much memory or system resources, particularly when performing a deep scan of a hard drive. Users should do some research and read reviews before investing in any software solution. *This book will highlight many programs and also offer a great Web site to review the latest software in Chapter 11.*

Even if a computer does not have antivirus software installed, users can scan a system for viruses and malware by using available online virus and malware scanners that can search your system for viruses and malware. Three are:

- Norton Security Scan (**http://security.symantec.com/sscv6/ WelcomePage.asp**)
- Panda Active Scan (**www.pandasecurity.com/activescan/**)
- Windows Live OneCare Safety Scanner (**http://onecare. live.com/site/en-us/default.htm**)

The following checklist will help users ensure their computers are optimally protected from virus infections:

- Keep antivirus software updated.
- Scan for viruses routinely.
- Use a personal firewall.
- Use antispyware software.
- Keep operating system patches up to date.
- Use antispam software.
- Do not open e-mail attachments unless they are from trusted sources.
- Constantly be on the lookout for phishing e-mails.
- Be wary of e-mail hoaxes.

Luckily, antivirus software does much more than defend against viruses and identify them when they are found on a system. One of the most powerful features of antivirus software is its ability to remove viruses from a computer. Antivirus software must be configured to scan all incoming and outgoing e-mail attachments. This is typically the default setting.

Additionally, users must configure antivirus software to scan their entire systems periodically. It is best to scan the entire system for viruses and malware at least weekly. Ideally, antivirus software should scan the boot sector of the hard drive upon start up to ensure that viruses have not infected the boot sector of a computer. Again, most of this is included in modern antivirus software.

Chinese Internet security provider Kingsoft reported in October 2009 that 3,031,921 new viruses were detected in mainland China and 20,812,698 computers were affected by these viruses, all within a month. Additionally, the site stated that more than 1.2 million Web sites were infected with Trojans. This shows that the threat of computer viruses is real and users must take Internet security seriously.

An antivirus program will inspect every file, folder, hard disk, and removable media, including flash drives and SD cards, in a computer to check for viruses. If users are installing antivirus software onto a computer that has accessed the Internet unprotected, they should expect it to find viruses. Antivirus software then works in the background, checking incoming and outgoing e-mail attachments for viruses, scans downloaded files, and constantly looks for virus signatures. With antivirus software continuously examining computers with the most recent updates, users are well protected. But they should remember that new viruses and variants of old viruses are "released into the wild" every day.

Viruses and Trojans have signatures or recognizable signs that antivirus software uses to detect them. When antivirus software is updated with the most recent signatures to detect all known viruses the software compares the files and folders from a user's computer against its signature database for a match. A match would mean the computer has a virus, which can usually be removed by the antivirus software. Unfortunately, as good as antivirus software is, significantly more advanced viruses are created every day. These viruses might be undetectable or constantly morph to hide from discovery. For example, polymorphic viruses change their code or appearance automatically, evading detection while still delivering their malicious payload.

Antivirus software manufacturers also identify viruses by recording data about critical system files and the windows registry and store this information so it can be constantly looked at and compared against the system files to ensure they have not been altered or replaced. With the heuristic scanning technique, the software detects viruses based on recognition of a signature or a piece of software code that might have characteristics similar to those of viruses. In other words, the antivirus software examines files for indicators of a certain virus. Heuristic scanning looks at files and code for variation or deviation from normal or expected code, indicating the possibility of a virus. This allows for detection of viruses before they might even be reported or before an antivirus software manufacturer has released updates to combat and remove the virus. The disadvantage is that this is not an exact science, and scanning might identify perfectly safe, legitimate files as viruses.

In most cases, antivirus software is not built to remove infected files identified in a heuristic scan; therefore, computer users might want to submit the file for examination to the antivirus manufacturer or to another antivirus lab, such as Virus Total (**www.virus-total.com**), a company that analyzes suspicious files.

As mentioned previously, computer users should schedule scans at least weekly on their computers. It is best to set the scan to run at a time and date when the computer might not be needed for other services, because a full scan can be both time and resource intensive. Users should be sure they do not schedule scans during periods when their computers are normally turned off or in sleep mode, as this will prevent the scan from running.

Viruses can destroy, alter, delete, or damage files. Removing invasive viruses might also damage operating system files. Users must be prepared for computer failure — caused by viruses, hard drive failure, or other events — at all times. It is critical computer users make routine backups of critical data. They should constantly back up all personal data, including documents, databases, Web sites, e-mails, financial data, music, and photographs. It is a good idea to use both an external hard drive as well as an online backup service, such as Carbonite, which safely stores data in an offsite location. The service performs backups incrementally when users' computers are idle and every time they update their computers. Backup services might be the best investment computer users can make in data protection and security.

If antivirus software is ineffective in removing viruses or an operating system has become damaged beyond repair, will not boot, or will not function properly, computer users have a few options, one of which is professional antivirus removal assistance. Many services, such as PC UltraCare (**http://pcultracare.com**), will attempt to remotely access and remove viruses from a computer.

Webroot (**www.webroot.com**) offers remote diagnostics for virus and spyware removal. The typical service costs less than $50 for the diagnosis and another $50 for removal services. Most of these services require the ability to connect to an infected PC remotely. If users do not have this capability because the virus or malware damaged the operating system, users can use a local computer repair technician to service their machines. In most cases, antivirus specialists will run a variety of malware and virus removal software applications on a computer, but if users can boot their PCs, they can do the same thing for free.

If a computer is infected to the point that the user cannot restore it to its original state or the damage is widespread, he or she will have to re-install the operating system. If users must do this, they should ensure they do a clean installation, which will completely reformat and wipe out all data on the hard drive. A user needs good backups of his or her data and the software installation disks to perform the installations. This process might be time-consuming and a bit of a hassle, but it ensures a computer is free of malware and viruses.

If a user does not have a good backup, he or she must extract critical data from the hard drive before reinstalling the operating system. If the user can boot the computer, he or she can usually transfer files — such as photographs, financial documents, music, and other important data — to an external hard drive or flash drive, so the user can restore it after reinstalling the operating system. If a computer is damaged to the point that it cannot boot into Windows, users can try to recover data by removing the internal hard drive and installing it into another computer as a secondary drive (non-boot drive) and then moving it off the damaged drive to another hard drive. You could also install the internal hard drive into an external hard drive enclosure (available at most major computer stores), plug it into another computer through a USB or FireWire port, and recover the data by simply copying it from the old drive to the new drive. Users should make sure the computer they plug this drive into has updated antivirus and antimalware installed and that it scans the hard drive upon recognition to prevent the spread of any infection to the new computer. Overall, this is a simple operation; however, you can also seek out the assistance of your local computer repair technician to recover data from damaged hard drives.

For users who cannot accomplish this, a local computer repair technician should be able to recover their data. Because many viruses are destructive in nature, there is a real possibility the virus might have destroyed data, reformatted the hard drive, or rendered data unrecoverable. Therefore, it is critical users maintain good backups at all times. This is important for more than just viruses and malware; good backups protect data in case of fire, flooding, theft, earthquake, hurricane, tornado, power surge, or other natural or manmade disasters. There are specialty companies that can attempt data recovery from corrupted hard drives if the file system is deleted, damaged, and sometimes even if erased. These services are highly specialized and very expensive. Maintaining good backups is the best way to protect data for a quick recovery.

Keep in mind the purpose of viruses is to replicate and spread, negatively affecting computer or network performance; however, they typically do not destroy operating systems. Why? The reason is simple, viruses are designed to replicate and spread. If they crash a computer, they cannot replicate or spread. A damaged, impaired, infected computer might suffer tremendous performance reductions and critical data or files might be altered or destroyed, but if the computer keeps running, it keeps spreading the virus. Obviously, this is just a generalization, as there are many viruses that replicate and spread and then damage or destroy their host after they have spread.

Again, prevention is the best form of attack against viruses and malware. Block the virus and you win. Computer users must always keep their guards up at all times and be wary of their actions while on the Internet. Social networking sites are incredibly popular, and just like the Internet, are fraught with peril of viruses and hoaxes. There has been an increase in the number of potential viruses and hoaxes found throughout these popular sites. For example, some social networking site members might have received e-mails asking them to click on a link to view an awesome movie. The message then might have infected their computers with the Koobface virus. This message, looking very much like a standard e-mail from the social networking site, is delivered through e-mail and invites recipients to check out the video through a hyperlink. When the link is clicked, nothing nefarious seems to happen; instead the recipient is prompted to update his or her "flash" player so the video file can play. The computer user launches the file "flash_player.exe" and the virus is launched. This particular virus will turn a PC into a bot that eventually joins a botnet.

This virus was clever; how could the recipient have detected it? Computer users should review the e-mail carefully; does it look authentic? They should look at the URL of the hyperlink; is it really taking them to the social networking site? Are there spelling errors or other obvious mistakes in the e-mail? If in doubt, do not click. If it was a legitimate message members could read the message after logging into their accounts. Computer users should open a new browser window and log in securely. If there is no message when the user logs in, this proves that the e-mail was a virus, phishing, or malware attack.

Another popular Facebook e-mail is Bredolab, which comes as a legitimate-looking "password reset" e-mail. If users click on the "Forgot Password" link, they are sent a file to reset their passwords. Users might be concerned their passwords are being compromised after receiving this e-mail that they did not initiate. Many users will open the file, launching the virus. Bredolab is a nasty Trojan that will automatically install software from the Internet onto a PC. It also modifies critical Windows system files. How does one avoid this virus infection? If a user did not request a password reset, he or she should not be getting a password reset notification, so the user should not open it. Users who did request new passwords will not get it as an attachment to an e-mail. One should never open an attachment to an e-mail that is not from a trusted source.

Sometimes, even the best antivirus programs are only partially successful in detecting and removing threats. Doing research and comparing the features and capabilities of antivirus programs will help ensure users choose the best product for their particular needs. There are differences between antivirus software; most will detect common viruses, some work better than others on heuristic viruses, but some might catch less than half of the threats that are roaming the Internet. Newer virus-detection methods send suspected infected files to a "cloud" computer, where it will be checked by various antivirus programs. That method is desirable because antivirus programs can only check one signature at a time per file and might take longer to respond to an emerging threat. A cloud computer is a new way of sharing resources for the common goal of stopping and eliminating viruses and malware by sharing large antivirus resources. Panda Security is one of the companies that features "cloud technology." Cloud technology antivirus solutions feature detection of viruses through a series of antivirus "cloud" Internet servers, enabling users to use many servers to concurrently scan, detect, and combat viruses. Panda Security has a free cloud antivirus that you can download and install on your computer available at: **www.cloudantivirus. com/en**.

On any new computer, one of the first things users must do is install a reputable antivirus software program. Second, they must ensure all operating system patches have been installed. Those who have a personal computer or small-business network have less of a possibility of being attacked if they use antivirus and antimalware programs. In a public network or even on a corporate network, there are many computers and individuals whom users cannot control, thus the threats increase exponentially. One person's mistake can infect an entire network, causing a company to lose plenty of data and productivity due to the unintentional release of a virus or malware into the network.

Those who operate a home or small-business network must ensure all computers are protected 24/7. If remote access — file sharing or other methods in which a network is accessed by external computers the user has no control over — is necessary, users must ensure their networks are fully protected against viruses and spyware. Most companies provide free antivirus software for business and personal use to minimize their exposure to risk from their own employees. Of course, many programs are already free and highly effective.

Computer users need to ensure they have an updated copy of antivirus software installed on every computer, whether it is part of a network or not. Viruses can also be transmitted over floppy disks, hard drives, CDs, DVDs, and flash drives. An attacker will search for the weakest link in a computer network and exploit it, so users need to ensure each computer system is secure and protected at all times. The type of antivirus program a user chooses will play a big part in how secure a business network will be. Users might feel their personal computers are protected with antivirus software that only relies on signature-based technology. On the other hand, in a larger business network, computers need antivirus software able to detect, catch, and contain the newest forms of viruses using heuristic technology. If a computer user is running a small business, he or she might wish to limit employee access to critical system files and data to prevent accidental or intentional damage or release of an infection into the network.

Business managers need to make sure both they and employees know to stay away from suspicious e-mail attachments and to scan them first with an antivirus program. Viruses are typically spread via attachments to e-mails or through security holes in unpatched operating systems. For a computer to be infected with a virus, users typically need to open those e-mail attachments or sometimes just the e-mail, which activates the virus attached to it.

Another important thing to do is to make sure that a computer is not already infected with a virus program by scanning it with an updated antivirus application or one of the free online scanners mentioned in this book. When a virus gets into a user's computer, it slowly spreads by copying itself to parts of the files on the computer. Users might need to consider disabling Flash, JavaScript, and Java programs in a Web browser. These programs start automatically and might activate or spread a virus, particularly through automatic downloads.

Computer users should be on the lookout constantly for any changes in their computers' performance. Users should check for symptoms of a virus infection. Changes in file size, system performance, resource utilization, and available hard drive space are some of the indications of a potential infection. Changes to how a computer boots, sudden rebooting or crashing of the computer, as well as system lockup or freezing are all signs of viruses or other system problems. Also, if users notice a sudden inability to find certain devices that are connected to a computer, such as a printer or external drive, or if the computer system does not find or does not allow a user to access certain parts of the computer system, such as folders and hard drives, this might indicate a virus or malware infection.

Other symptoms that tell users that a computer is infected with a computer virus are distortions, either in the computer screen or various parts of a computer system. This might appear in menus where things have changed location or disappeared or in the appearance of occasional error messages during attempts to do routine operations.

If a deep search using an antivirus program yields no positive results, users might be dealing with a brand new virus or with a new variation of a previous virus that has not yet been detected. A computer user needs to know where to look and what to do to get rid of it as soon as possible, before it destroys any more personal data. Typically antivirus software manufacturers are quick to release updates to combat newly detected viruses. For stubborn or complex viruses, they might develop tools or removal programs specifically for that individual virus threat.

Another way is to protect a computer system is to use strong passwords. Users should make sure they never reveal passwords to other people. Businesses should make sure they disable user accounts and change passwords after an employee leaves the business, so he or she will not have access to the computer any longer. This seems obvious, but many businesses' former employees still have access to sensitive data and computer networks because their access was never terminated; it is critical to terminate access for departed employees immediately. Employees should know to never disclose their password to anyone outside of the company. Employees should choose long passwords that are a combination of letters, numbers, and signs. Passwords should be gibberish, not a combination of words, and should contain no personal data, such as an ID or a birth date. Another way to secure a network is to encrypt hard drives. This ensures data is impossible to read without proper credentials. Family members — especially teenagers — or employees should know that downloading and installing the wrong piece of software could endanger the entire network and possibly compromise sensitive information by releasing a virus or malware.

If an antivirus scanner detects a virus that it cannot remove, there might be other tools that can remove the virus. There are many resources available on the Internet to report viruses, research viruses, view the current threat level, read about new viruses, and get the latest advice in preventing viruses from infecting computers or networks. These sites also boast information about removal techniques and many offer free removal tools for specific viruses. There are dozens of high quality antivirus software applications available. *Many of the top performers are listed in Chapter 11, which will be a handy reference guide as you choose which security software to use on your computers and networks.* If an antivirus program cannot remove a virus, it is possible a different antivirus application might be able to remove it; therefore, doing research on the following sites, or through Web searches about a specific virus, might help a computer user find a rapid solution to clean the infected computer.

- The Symantec AntiVirus Research Center (SARC) hosts the Symantec Internet Threat Meter, which measures the current threats against e-mail, Internet activity, instant messaging, and file sharing. SARC is a great resource to research viruses, characteristics, and removal techniques. The basic home user site is **www.symantec.com/norton/security_response/index.jsp**. The more advanced and recommended business site is **www.symantec.com/business/security_response/index.jsp**.

- The Panda Security blog, at **http://pandalabs.pandasecurity.com**, is a wealth of information, including breaking security news. PandaLabs works to identify and defeat spyware and malware worldwide. Their site is located at

www.pandasecurity.com/homeusers/security-info/pandalabs. Panda also hosts a real-time virus threat list at **www.pandasecurity.com/homeusers/security-info/latest-threats**.

- McAfee also has a site rich with information on the latest threats. It features global maps to monitor virus outbreaks, top threats, tracking tools, and free removal tools. Users can visit the McAfee site at **http://home.mcafee.com/VirusInfo**. The McAfee Threat Center has breaking news on security-related matters. Users can find it at **www.mcafee.com/us/threat_center/default.asp**.

- The TrendMicro Threat Encyclopedia is an update date source for the latest security, malware, and other online threats. The encyclopedia is located at **http://threatinfo.trendmicro.com/vinfo.**

- The CA Virus Information Center is a complete resource for protecting home and business computer systems against malware. It provides the latest in security threats and removal and reporting tools. The CA Virus Information Center Web site is located at **www.ca.com/us/anti-virus.aspx**.

A great source of information related to viruses is Panda Security's weekly report on viruses and intruders. This is a free, weekly e-mail summary of the latest virus threats. Users can sign up for these e-mail alerts through Panda Security at **www.pandasecurity.com**. Here is a sample report:

PANDA SECURITY'S WEEKLY REPORT ON VIRUSES AND INTRUDERS

Virus Alerts, by Panda Security (**www.pandasecurity.com**)

This week, the PandaLabs report presents two new Trojans that try to trick users to steal their data.

FakeWindows.A is a Trojan that resembles a Windows XP activation process (see image here, via Flickr: **www.flickr.com/photos/ panda_security/4174519256**).

This malware can reach computers through e-mail or can be downloaded from a malicious Web page. It tries to get users to believe that the operating system is requesting their data to activate the account (see image here, via Flickr: **www.flickr.com/ photos/panda_security/4173761047/**).

In addition to personal data, the Trojan also requests bank details. On entering them, the program displays an error screen indicating it was impossible to connect to the server. Consequently, in addition to making data theft easier, users' computers are blocked.

On the other hand, the UrlDistract.A Trojan reaches computers through e-mails with an icon that resembles a video. When run, the Trojan silently steals users' information while it distracts them by opening a YouTube video called "Little Superstar," where an actor dances to music (see image here, via Flickr: **www.flickr.com/photos/panda_security/4173761103**). The Trojan then connects to an address in Atlanta (USA) and sends all the data stolen from the computer.

More information about these and other malicious codes is available in the Panda Security Encyclopedia, **www.pandasecurity. com/homeusers/security-info**.

You can also follow Panda Security's online activity on its Twitter page: **http://twitter.com/Panda_Security**, and PandaLabs blog: **www.pandalabs.com**

Reprinted with Permission, Panda Security, Inc.

CHAPTER 4

Spam, Spoofing, Phishing, & E-Mail Hoaxes: What They Are and How to Block Them

E-mail spam is the sending of unsolicited commercial e-mail messages to many recipients. Many spammers buy bulk e-mail addresses from disreputable resellers or through a variety of means, such as harvesting them from online forums, domain name listings, or Web pages. They might also include commonly used e-mail addresses, such as sales@, admin@, support@, or service@, with a user's domain or use specialized Web spider software to steal e-mail addresses from Web sites and other lists. E-mail harvesting occurs when spammers use third-party software to search the Internet and "harvest" or steal e-mail addresses from Web pages and collect them in a database. These harvested e-mail addresses can amount to millions of e-mails that are in turn used for unsolicited bulk spam e-mails.

Spoofed e-mails, virus attachments, phishing, and e-mail hoaxes are ways in which malicious attackers can harm, manipulate, or destroy a computer system or network and cause financial harm on unsuspecting and unprepared users. These attacks are mainly used to profit at the expense of the users or to gain personal and private information, which is used to attain money through various means or perform other harmful activities, such as identify theft.

Phishing and spoofing are commonly confused with one another. Phishing will typically use spoofing techniques; however, spoofing is not necessarily considered to be phishing. Spoofing occurs when one impersonates an individual or business to trick an unsuspecting user into doing something. Typically, spoofing is designed to get a user to click a link to download a malware file, launch a virus, or perform another malicious attack. Phishing entails attacks in which the sender attempts to extract sensitive information, typically financial, from the user. This is often done with a spoofed e-mail and spoofed Web site that looks authentic and is used to steal login and password information for online bank accounts. Spoofed e-mails are typically designed to cause malicious damage to a computer or network, whereas phishing e-mails are designed to steal personal information for financial gain.

Spoofing

A major form of spam is the "spoofing" of e-mail addresses. Spoofing is a method of concealing the identity of the sender and making the recipient believe the e-mail is from a reputable business or trusted individual. With spoofing, the spammer modifies the e-mail message so it appears to have come from another e-mail account that the Internet user trusts. Spoofing can occur with any e-mail account or domain name. For example, a user might get an e-mail from Bruce Brown with the e-mail address of bruce@brucecbrown.com. This is a legitimate e-mail account and avoids spam filters. It gives the recipient peace of mind because he or she knows this e-mail is from someone the user knows and trusts, yet spoofed e-mails are often malicious and can fool the recipient into thinking they are trusted, legitimate e-mails. Attackers spoof e-mails to create a false sense of security at the receiver's end so the user is less cautious than usual when opening and reading the e-mail.

Spoofing can cause a multitude of security and other problems. A user can become bombarded by spoofed e-mails, many of which appear to be legitimate. Dealing with spoofed e-mails is frustrating and time-consuming. As a Web site or domain name owner it is much worse; typically bounced e-mails are sent back to the spoofed domain e-mail account — the owner's. Owners might find they are receiving replies, bounced e-mails, and negative replies for an e-mail that they never sent. Spoofed e-mails aim to release privacy information or passwords to third parties who will use them against a business. Those who suspect spoofing of their e-mail accounts or want more detailed information about spoofing should contact the Cert Coordination Center at **www. cert.org**. The CERT® Coordination Center, located at Carnegie Mellon University's Software Engineering Institute, studies Internet security vulnerabilities, researches long-term changes in networked systems, and develops information and training to improve computer and network security. Spoofed e-mails as well as spam e-mails are common sources for the transfer of viruses and other malware programs.

Most spammers are after privacy and/or financial data. Their e-mails often offer illicit activities, such as pornography, get-rich-quick schemes, pirated software, or overseas business scams. The best combatant against spam is antispam filters, junk mail filters, and specialized software for the e-mail server and the mail client to protect e-mail accounts. These will be discussed in detail later in this chapter. This chapter will also show computer users how to protect themselves and defend against spam.

There are ways to identify a spoofed e-mail and there are steps users can take to ensure they are protected, but these security measures require attentiveness and alertness. Computer users should always make sure they check senders' e-mail addresses to validate that the address is from the actual company Web site. This in itself does not mean the e-mail is not a phishing e-mail, but it helps to validate the e-mail address. Users should check the domain name and e-mail address to protect against letter substitution, which is a technique where one letter in an e-mail address or domain name is replaced so it looks similar to the authentic e-mail address or domain name (for example, gma1l.com for gmail. com).

Criminals commonly use similar-sounding domain names posing as legitimate e-mails or Web sites. Users also need to check the contents of e-mails. They should check if the graphics vary from the graphics on the company's Web site. The graphics can vary by color, location, lack of details, quality of details, and size. Spoofed e-mail graphics might be blurry, inaccurate, faded, or pixilated. Users should also pay attention to grammar and spelling mistakes in the e-mail, as well as to the tone of e-mail. Companies hire professional people to write their e-mails, so spelling and grammar mistakes in a legitimate e-mail are a rarity, and the tone of voice is professional and businesslike. Small changes in words that indicate the writer is not a native American English speaker (for example using colour instead of color) might indicate a spoof.

There are also other ways to spot a spoofed e-mail. The user can go to the legitimate Web site from which the e-mail allegedly came, check the domain name of the e-mail Web site, and compare. Again, a user should never click on any links in an e-mail that purports to take a recipient to a site to log in or update personal or financial information. Instead, computer users should open a new browser window and navigate to the proper Web site if they wish to log in. One should never open attachments to e-mails unless it is certain they are from legitimate sources and only if the user has active, updated antivirus and antimalware software installed.

Phishing

Another major threat is phishing. Phishing is a variation on the word "fishing," which means that "phishers" will throw out baited Web sites, hoping someone will "bite." Phishing attacks can be launched via e-mail or instant messenger. Phishing is the sending of an e-mail to another e-mail account where the sender attempts to impersonate a legitimate company or individual in an attempt to trick the recipient into divulging privacy information that will be used for identity theft. The e-mail directs users to visit a Web site where they are asked to update personal information, such as passwords and credit card, social security, and bank account numbers the legitimate organization already has. The Web site, however, is bogus and set up only to steal the users' information.

For example, a common phishing scheme involves receiving e-mails purporting to be from a reputable source stating that you must access your account to update credit card or contact information or perform other actions. Unsuspecting individuals are taken to a site that looks just like the real site, but it is not. When the user enters the spoof site, he or she is giving away his or her user name and password. Although eBay, PayPal, and other Internet businesses have launched massive campaigns to educate their clients on potential phishing attempts, people still fall for phishing scams every day. The easiest way to avoid phishing scams is to never click on any links in any suspect e-mails. A user can also usually hover his or her mouse pointer over the embedded hyperlink in the e-mails. By looking at the actual URL — usually seen in the lower left hand corner of the Microsoft Outlook or Mozilla Thunderbird window when hovering the mouse over the link — users can often detect that it is fraudulent, although it is usually a close variant of the proper URL.

Reputable companies that are usually trusted sources, such as banks and e-commerce sites, are routinely targets of phishing scams. Banks have a considerable amount of experience in their business and they safeguard physical property and data behind secure vaults and strong network defenses. They also defend sensitive information and property, which, if damaged or stolen, can severely impact an individual's life. Many online users have some form of online banking access. To attract customers, many banks allow users to access their accounts via the Internet from any computer system, located anywhere in the world, and thus are ideal targets for phishing schemes. Criminals might use e-mails, which look exactly like the recipient's own bank's e-mails, typically asking the recipient to register his or her account, log in to the system, update a password, or re-enter personal information. Typically these phishing schemes do not involve transferring money or providing account number details, because the goal is to capture users' account login and password information, giving the criminal full access to their bank accounts.

Phishing schemes vary from updating a password to messages that the bank's computer system accidentally destroyed some users' passwords and/or data, and the users need to enter the bank's Web site and enter their details again to re-store them. The user will navigate to the "bank" Web site using the hyperlink provided in the e-mail. This link leads users to a Web site that looks almost exactly like the legitimate company's Web site. The unsuspecting users will believe these phishing e-mails are all legitimate and attempt to log in or change their password. When they do this, their login and password information is captured by the criminals. Sometimes the Web site will notify the users that the action was completed and redirect them to the real Web site so the phishing will go undetected. The criminals will quickly use this login information to access the user's online bank accounts and change the passwords, locking out the account owner.

In many cases, the phishing e-mail uses images, fonts, colors, and designs taken from actual bank e-mails so they look authentic. By the time most users figure out what happened, it is too late. The criminals have already accessed their financial accounts and started the process to transfer money to other accounts, make online purchases, and commit other fraudulent activity.

Most modern antivirus software not only scans for viruses, but also for spoofed e-mails and phishing attacks. Computer users can further defend against these attacks by using common sense and some investigative techniques. First, if a user gets e-mails from banks, e-commerce, and other sites, he or she should not click the links. Instead, the user should open a new browser window, navigate to that site, and log in directly, avoiding any potential of clicking on a phishing link. Criminals might use similar domain names to trick users into believing a phishing site is legitimate or use an alternate domain name extension, such as mybank.net instead of mybank.com. Criminals might attempt to trick people by varying letters within a domain name where the average user might not notice the subtle change, such as **www. bankofamerlca.com**, where the URL uses a "1" instead of "I" in the word "America." Attackers might also purchase the same exact Web site name but under a different domain name; e.g.: **www. bankofamerica.co.uk** instead of **www.bankofamerica.com**.

Big, trustworthy Web sites are often owned by large companies that have branches all over the world, or deal with customers from all over the world. So it is reasonable to believe they might have a different domain name for customers from a different country, to customize the Web site to those people or to remove clutter by removing any irrelevant information. For example, Google deals with people all over the world, so it is reasonable to believe they registered Google with various domain names extensions. Because of legal issues in some countries, Google had to register itself or part of its services under different names, such as Google Mail instead of Gmail, etc.

The key difference between operating legal, permission-based e-mail marketing campaigns and spam is the use of "opt-in" e-mail lists. Spam or junk e-mail is e-mail that is sent to one or more recipients who did not request it, whereas double opt-in e-mail lists are considered legal because the recipients had to request to be on the list and validate that request before receiving any e-mails.

Whaling

Whaling is very similar to other forms of e-mail attacks, except that these target corporate executives. Attackers find the names and e-mail addresses of these executive and create authentic-looking, personalized e-mails to them. Instead of a "canned" e-mail, they are customized to the recipient's company and position within that company. The volume of whaling e-mails is much lower than typical spam, phishing, or spoofing e-mails, but it is highly effective. The desired actions are the same as in other e-mail scams: get the e-mail recipient to click on an embedded link, install malware or spyware on his or her machine, and install keyloggers or other software to exploit and steal personal and/or financial data. Often these e-mails are created to appear as if they came from the Better Business Bureau, advising the executive of a complaint, to which he or she must respond. Others might appear to be a corporate hotline, vendor, or corporate recruiter.

Pharming

Just like with real fishing, in computer phishing criminals cast out some lines and hope for a few nibbles, eventually snagging a few takers. Pharming, like farming, refers to a hacker harvesting large yields from a wide population of people who legitimately believe they are on the real Web site entering login credentials. Pharming is very similar to phishing, in that a user is unknowingly redirected to a fraudulent Web site to conduct transactions. The key difference is that pharming involves actually modifying the host file on a computer or wireless router by installing malware or exploiting known vulnerabilities in domain name servers (DNS) and redirecting the user to a fraudulent Web site without his or her knowledge or consent. This malware is often passed through e-mail and can even work through Java applets or JavaScript downloads on Web pages.

Pharming modifies the host record IP address of Web site and redirects computer users to the IP address of a fraudulent Web site without their knowledge. This is much more effective than phishing because the user actually typed in the *correct* domain name for the Web site they wanted to visit. This is typically done through DNS cache poisoning. DNS translate IP addresses into a domain name. It is easy to remember Amazon.com, but what is the IP address for Amazon.com? DNS servers do the work for Internet users by converting the domain name into the IP address, and lookup what Web server the site is physically hosted on, directing Web surfers to that server to access the Web site via their Web browser. DNS cache poisoning lets the hacker change this system and redirect legitimate Web site traffic to a fraudulent Web site, even though the domain name in the browser is correct. Pharming can be extraordinarily damaging and can affect large groups of people.

CAN-SPAM Act

According to the Federal Trade Commission (FTC), The Controlling the Assault of Non-Solicited Pornography and Marketing (CAN-SPAM) Act of 2003 establishes requirements for those who send commercial e-mail, spells out penalties for spammers and companies whose products are advertised in spam if they violate the law, and gives consumers the right to ask e-mailers to stop spamming them. The law, which became effective Jan. 1, 2004, covers e-mail whose primary purpose is advertising or promoting a commercial product or service, including content on a Web site. A "transactional or relationship message" e-mail — a message that facilitates an agreed-upon transaction or updates a customer in an existing business relationship — may not contain false or misleading routing information, but otherwise is exempt from most provisions of the CAN-SPAM Act, according to the FTC. The FTC, the nation's consumer protection agency, is authorized to enforce the CAN-SPAM Act. CAN-SPAM also gives the Department of Justice (DOJ) the authority to enforce its criminal sanctions. Other federal and state agencies can enforce the law against organizations under their jurisdiction and companies that provide Internet access may sue violators as well.

The following section provides a detailed look at the CAN-SPAM Act.

CAN-SPAM Act requirements

Bans false or misleading header information

An e-mail's "From," "To," and routing information — including the originating domain name and e-mail address — must be accurate and identify the person who initiated the e-mail.

Prohibits deceptive subject lines

The subject line cannot mislead the recipient about the contents or subject matter of the message.

Requires that an e-mail give recipients an opt-out method

E-mail senders must provide a return e-mail address or another Internet-based response mechanism that allows a recipient to ask them not to send future e-mail messages to that e-mail address. Senders must honor the requests. Senders may create a "menu" of choices to allow a recipient to opt out of certain types of messages, but they must include the option to end any commercial messages from the sender. Any opt-out mechanism the e-mail offers must be able to process opt-out requests for at least 30 days after the commercial e-mail is sent. When a sender receives an opt-out request, the law gives the sender ten business days to stop e-mailing the requestor's e-mail address. The sender cannot help another entity send e-mail to that address or have another entity send e-mail on the original sender's behalf to that address. Finally, it is illegal for an individual or organization to sell or transfer the e-mail addresses of people who choose not to receive a sender's e-mail, even in the form of a mailing list, unless the sender transfers the addresses to another entity that can comply with the law. This means that your e-mail address cannot be legally sold to anyone else unless you have given that person permission to use your e-mail address and the buyer of the mailing list complies with all spam laws.

State it is an advertisement and include an address

Commercial e-mail messages must contain a clear and conspicuous notice that the message is an advertisement or solicitation and that the recipient can opt out of receiving more commercial e-mail from the sender. It also must include the sender's valid physical postal address.

Penalties for each violation of the CAN-SPAM Act are subject to fines of up to $16,000. Deceptive commercial e-mail also is subject to laws banning false or misleading advertising. Additional fines are provided for commercial e-mailers who not only violate the rules described previously, but also:

- "Harvest" e-mail addresses from Web sites or Web services that have published a notice prohibiting the transfer of e-mail addresses for the purpose of sending e-mail.

- Generate e-mail addresses using a "dictionary attack" — combining names, letters, or numbers into multiple permutations.

- Use scripts or other automated ways to register for multiple e-mail or user accounts to send commercial e-mail.

- Relay e-mails through a computer or network without permission — for example, by taking advantage of open relays or open proxies without authorization.

The law allows the Department of Justice to seek criminal penalties, including imprisonment, for commercial e-mailers who do or conspire to:

- Use another computer without authorization and send commercial e-mail from or through it.

- Use a computer to relay or retransmit multiple commercial e-mail messages to deceive or mislead recipients or an Internet access service about the origin of the message.

- Falsify header information in multiple e-mail messages and initiate the transmission of such messages.

- Register for multiple e-mail accounts or domain names using information that falsifies the identity of the actual registrant.

- Falsely represent themselves as owners of multiple Internet Protocol(IP) addresses that are used to send commercial e-mail messages.

The FTC has issued additional rules under the CAN-SPAM Act involving the required labeling of sexually explicit commercial e-mail and the criteria for determining "the primary purpose" of a commercial e-mail. See the FTC Web site at **www.ftc.gov/spam** for updates on implementation of the CAN-SPAM Act.

Most recipients of bulk e-mail, spam, or unsolicited advertisements view the messages as unwelcome, unpleasant, or offensive. However, there are many mailing lists that deliver solicited (opt-in), useful information to recipients based on a variety of subjects in which they have expressed an interest. In these cases, recipients have given their permission to allow companies to add their e-mail address to bulk mailing lists. Not all e-mail is spam; however, all spam is illegal and potentially harmful.

Analysts at Ferris Research estimated that spam would cost more than $130 billion worldwide and more than $42 billion in the United States in 2009, a more than 100 percent increase since 2005. How does spam cost money? Aside from the damage incurred from virus- or malware-infected spam, it dramatically impacts recipients in other measurable ways, such as productivity lost reading, sorting, and deleting spam e-mails; additional costs for software and hardware to combat spam; and increased costs for IT support to combat, deter, and remove spam. Spam's direct effects include the consumption of computer and network resources and the cost in human time and attention for dismissing unwanted messages. There are also costs incurred by the victims of spamming, such as financial data integrity, data theft, data destruction, pornography, and of course, virus and malware infection. Companies have lost money and data integrity because their employees have fallen for spam, spoofs, and phishing schemes by giving out sensitive company data, credit card information, or bank account numbers.

Recipients might find their inboxes full of spam, preventing them from receiving legitimate e-mails that cannot get to an inbox due to the overload of spam.

Spam filters often work too well, deleting important e-mails that they believe are spam. Users do have some control over filters by adjusting the settings — typically low, medium, or high — and most spam filters allow you to specify e-mail addresses and domains to automatically categorize as legitimate e-mails or as spam.

The CAN-SPAM Act gives recipients the right to stop unsolicited e-mails and spells out tough penalties for violations. The CAN-SPAM Act does not apply just to bulk e-mail; it also applies to all commercial e-mail traffic. The law makes no exception for business-to-business e-mail; therefore, all commercial e-mail must comply with the law. If this is true, why do e-mail users get hundreds of spam e-mails every day? Despite the law, spamming is prolific and, as the volume of e-mail use grows like it has in the past ten years, the volume of spam has matched that growth rate. Also, a majority of spam is originated outside of the United States.

Many businesses ask if the CAN-SPAM Act applies to their business e-mails. The answer depends on the primary purpose of the e-mail. An e-mail can contain three different types of information:

- **Commercial**: Advertises or promotes commercial products or services. This includes content from Web sites that are operated for commercial purposes.

- **Transactional or relationship**: Contains information on a previously agreed-upon transaction or updates customers about a previous or ongoing transaction.

- **Content**: E-mail that is neither commercial nor transactional or relationship. However, if this content primarily commercial in nature, it must comply with the CAN-SPAM Act. This is how "personal" e-mail is excluded from the CAN-SPAM Act.

If an e-mail contains only transactional or relationship content, and its primary purpose is transactional or relationship, then it may not contain false or misleading routing information, but is otherwise exempt from most provisions of the CAN-SPAM Act. A transactional or relationship e-mail is one that is comprised of content that:

- Confirms a commercial transaction that the recipient already has agreed to.

- Provides warranty, recall, safety, or security information about a product or service.

- Provides information about a change in terms or features or account balance information regarding a membership, subscription, account, loan, or other ongoing commercial relationship.

- Provides information about an employment relationship or employee benefits.

- Delivers goods or services as part of a transaction that the recipient already has agreed to.

E-mail recipients should be aware that there are additional rules that apply to the transmission of sexually explicit e-mail. Under the CAN-SPAM Act, e-mails with sexually oriented material must include the warning "SEXUALLY-EXPLICIT:" at the beginning of the subject line. In addition, the rule requires the electronic equivalent of a "brown paper wrapper" in the body of the message. When a recipient opens the message, the only things that may be viewable on the recipient's screen are the words "SEXUALLY-EXPLICIT;" and the same information required in any other commercial e-mail: a disclosure that the message is an ad, the sender's physical postal address, and the procedure for how recipients can opt out of receiving messages from this sender in the future. No graphics are allowed on the "brown paper wrapper," which is a cover to prevent viewing of the body of the e-mail. Recipients must not be able to view sexually explicit content without an affirmative act on their part, such as clicking on a hyperlink.

Hoaxes

E-mail hoaxes are prevalent, and most e-mail users likely have received their fair share of these spam e-mails. Hoaxes typically offer amazing financial awards, gifts, or other incentives. In return, they ask for the recipient's personally identifiable information, such as bank account and routing numbers or social security numbers. They might also require recipients to send money to someone in return for a large payout. These are hoaxes and scams.

Some might be disguised as a very legitimate-looking phishing e-mail from a legitimate individual or business, but more times than not, they are straight-forward e-mails with very specific instructions and a phone number to call or e-mail address to contact.

In an advance-fee fraud, an e-mail recipient sends a little money to someone who will send the recipient much larger sums of money in return for "helping" move money out of a foreign country or some other type of promise. The victim will have to send some money to initiate the transaction and often send more money over and over again to expedite the transaction. Once the victim is deeply embedded (and indebted), he or she never hears from the e-mail sender again. Hoax e-mails come in many forms, such as lottery winnings, inheritance notifications, messages from a long-lost relative who wants to send the recipient money, a plea for help from a deposed foreign national who secretly wants to move money into the United States, and nearly every other story imaginable. These are all hoaxes and they are illegal.

Stock hoaxes are very prevalent and many people fall for these hoaxes, losing millions of dollars annually. The premise is that the perpetrator buys low cost stock and then sends out millions of e-mails, which appear to be "confidential" in nature and not intended for public viewing, about the potential explosion in value of the stocks. Recipients buy the stocks because they are not overly expensive. Although buyers are investing in a legitimate company, this overinflates the stock values. As buyers invest, the stock becomes more and more valuable. The perpetrator then sells his or her stock at the higher prices and cashes in on the profits. Over time, the overinflated stock prices drop sharply and all the investors lose their money.

One widely used hoax is to ask the user for a small sum of money, to take care of lawyer fees and paperwork, so the attacker will be able to "release" money that is held for him or her in a will or a bank account. In return for the e-mail recipient's help, the attacker will return the investment with a significant payment. The amount the sender has is so enormous and the interest recipients are going to get back on their initial investments is so big, that people get tempted by the easy money, especially if the attacker assures the users their investments will be returned in just a few days. Quick and easy money is tempting and greed can make people blind to the implausibility of the situation and of the dangers in their actions. They want to believe it, so they do.

Other hoaxes are e-mails that pull at people's heart strings. These ask for money to get an operation for the e-mail author's young child. It is called a chain e-mail, and it is sent by the attacker to many people. Some people believe the contents of the e-mail are legitimate and send money, as well as forward the message on to their friends, family, and co-workers, further spreading the hoax. Chain e-mails are hoax e-mails sent to many people, who send the e-mail on to additional people and so on. These spam e-mails always continue to "infect" people's inboxes and they travel all over the world for many years.

Many hoaxes warn of viruses, even telling recipients to click on an attachment to install a "patch" on their computers to block the virus. The attachment is malware. Other e-mails are disguised as charity fundraisers, security warnings, lottery notifications, pranks, chain e-mails, polls, and more.

How does one protect oneself from these hoaxes? E-mail recipients should not give out personally identifiable information or bank account information to anyone, nor should they send money to individuals in return for promises of large payouts. It is best not to make financial decisions based on e-mails. E-mail users should employ common sense and antispam protection so they never have to even look at these malicious e-mails. A few great sources for more information on hoaxes are Hoax-Slayer (**www. hoax-slayer.com**) and Hoax Busters (**www.hoaxbusters.org**).

Spam Virus E-Mails

Virus attachments are files that contain viruses that people attach to e-mails. A basic rule of thumb is to never open or read e-mails with attached files, or only open them if they were requested. Some virus attachments are more sophisticated than others and are embedded in photos that are placed as part of the e-mail. When the recipient opens the e-mail the virus is activated automatically. Some e-mail software shows a preview of the e-mail to users, which is a helpful feature to have and speeds up the reading of e-mails, but it might also trigger the virus and most security experts recommend this feature be disabled. Users can prevent the execution of some of the e-mails with virus attachments by not allowing HTML code or other code to be interpreted, both via the Web browser and e-mail account by not allowing HTML-based e-mails or converting them to text-only mode.

Many spam e-mails that have a virus attachment are made to look like enticing get-rich-quick schemes, free sexual pictures (often of celebrities), or legitimate-looking e-mails. Most contain attachments asking the recipient to open them. Sometimes the message will be of a sexual nature or enticing in another way. The attackers entice recipients into opening the attachment and activating the virus. Usually computer users are safe by just not opening the e-mail. However, virus writers are becoming very sophisticated and users can sometimes activate viruses by simply reading or previewing the e-mail or clicking on it. Some e-mails with virus attachments add "RE:" to the title of the e-mail, which is a sign that indicates it is a response to an e-mail the victim sent. If users only take a quick glance at these messages they will probably open them, thinking it is a reply to something they might have sent; instead it is likely a spoofed e-mail from someone the recipient knows or an e-mail with a virus attached to it.

E-Mail Relaying

E-mail relaying is not quite as prevalent as it once was; however, it is still a widespread problem that exacerbates the spam problem and simplifies the proliferation of spam e-mails. An open relay is a mail server that allows anyone to send e-mail through it to any other e-mail destination. With an open relay, spammers use a victim's e-mail server to send their spam. E-mail servers allow an open relay when they are improperly configured or when a hacker has modified the system settings on the simple mail transfer protocol (SMTP) or mail server.

An open relay can be used to send out millions of e-mails per day. Victims likely will not even know it is happening to their systems. Spammers can hide because the victim's domain name mail server is actually sending the spam e-mails. The primary damage through open relays is the spam that is generated through them. However, collateral damage to the victim might include a loss in reputation if a domain is marked as a spammer and the victim's server IP address might even by blocked by Internet service providers.

Individuals and organizations can test their mail servers' IP addresses or domains at SpamHelp (**www.spamhelp.org**) to see if it is an open relay. If a mail server fails an open relay test, a user should consult with his or her technical support staff to block this or it will be exploited for spam. It is important to note that most commercial Web hosting services that also provide computer users with SMTP e-mail capability ensure users' Web servers and mail servers are secure and that relaying is blocked.

Spam Tools

Luckily there are numerous reputable resources available to assist computer users with identifying and combating spam, spoofing, and phishing. The following are some of them:

- Fight Spam on the Internet (**http://spam.abuse.net**): Contains an ongoing listing of spam related news, articles, and information.

- The Federal Trade Commission's Web site on spam (**www.ftc.gov/spam**): This site outlines the laws for consumers and businesses and the current penalties for violating antispam laws. On this site, individuals can file spam complaints; users just click on the "File a Complaint" link on the home page.

- Spam Laws (**www.spamlaws.com**): This site has all the most recent spam-related legislation and laws from the United States, Europe, and other countries, as well as state laws and selected case histories.

- The Coalition Against Unsolicited Commercial E-mail (**www.cauce.org**): A group whose primary purpose is to advocate for a legislative solution to the problem of unsolicited commercial e-mail.

- SpamCop (**www.spamcop.net**): This company determines the origin of unwanted e-mail and reports it to the relevant Internet service providers. Reporting unsolicited e-mail also helps feed spam filtering systems including SpamCop's own service.

In addition, there are several commercial or Web-based products that can help users combat spam. Some are listed below; however, Chapter 11 has a much more extensive guide:

- Vanquish Anti-Spam (**www.vanquish.com**)
- SpamButcher (**www.spambutcher.com**)
- InBoxer (**www.inboxer.com**)
- SpamBully (**www.spambully.com**)

Additionally, there are many reputable, free spam-blocker programs that will work with major e-mail applications. These include:

- MailWasher (**www.mailwasher.com**)
- Bullguard Spamfilter (**www.bullguard.com**)
- SpamFighter (**www.spamfighter.com**)
- SpamFence (**www.spamfence.net**)
- Spamihilator (**www.spamihilator.com**)

Additionally, many major antivirus packages contain some form of spam blockers. These packages include Panda Internet Security, McAfee Total Protection, TrendMicro Internet Security Pro and many others. The best antispam software is the one that delivers only the e-mails recipients want and blocks all of the e-mails they do not want. Unfortunately, even the best antispam software will let spam into an inbox, and even block valid e-mails that it believes to be spam. Some antispam solutions not only block specific e-mail addresses, but also search the subject lines and content text for spam indications. All antispam programs put suspected spam in a spam or junk folder so users can review it and mark it as either spam or safe so that it will be properly recognized in the future if there are other e-mails from the same sender.

Spam should be reported and it is simple to report spam. Unfortunately, most spam is never reported. Spam should be reported to the FTC by sending a copy of the unsolicited e-mail to spam@ uce.gov. E-mail users are also urged to send the e-mail to their Internet service providers, who typically have a standard e-mail address to report abuse, such as abuse@yourisp.com. This notifies them of the spam and they might take action to block that domain on their mail severs. When Internet users report spam they should include the full header of the offending e-mail. The "help" feature of their e-mail applications can give users instructions to retrieve the header of an e-mail. Typically this is done by right-clicking on the spam e-mail, clicking on properties, then details, and then message source or view source. Users can cut and paste this information into their e-mails' contents when reporting the spam.

Although there is a National Do Not Call Registry, there is no National Do Not E-mail Registry in the United States. There are some Web sites that appear to be "do not e-mail" registries; however, they are not legitimate. Internet users should not give these sites their e-mail addresses. E-mail users should protect their e-mail addresses when possible by not placing it on Web sites, blogs, and forums. Personal e-mail addresses should be kept private. Internet surfers should use a generic Yahoo! or Gmail account for their public interactions on blogs and other online forums. These can be easily discarded and changed if users find themselves bombarded with spam.

When a user receives spam e-mail, he or she should not respond to the messages. If the messages came to the main inbox, the user should mark them as spam and move them to the junk folder, blocking them from ever appearing again in the inbox. It is best to not reply nor ask to be "removed" from spam lists because this usually results in the recipient confirming the e-mail address as valid and only further exacerbates the problem as the e-mail is now used on even more spam bulk mailing lists.

Most Web-based e-mail applications have built-in spam filtering, which lets users customize the spam settings between no spam detection and very aggressive. The settings also lets users customize the action the spam filters take when spam is discovered. Aggressive settings might also tag legitimate e-mails as spam, so users should review their junk or spam e-mail folders.

Microsoft Outlook 2007 is one of the most widely used e-mail applications for home and business use. Outlook has built-in spam filtering options that let users customize and control what happens when spam is discovered. You can access this feature by clicking on the "Junk E-mail" button under the "Options" topic in the "Tools" menu at the toolbar at the top of the page.

Clicking on the "Junk E-mail" button gives users a wide variety of options, including the ability to turn off spam filtering or set the filtering default to low, high, or "safe-lists only," which means only e-mail on the user's safe sender list will get into the inbox. It also lets users choose how they want spam to be handled, such as permanently deleted, moved to a junk folder, and other warning options. Users can add safe senders and safe recipients. They can also explicitly block specific e-mail accounts and limit top-level domains for foreign e-mail accounts.

If spam does get through, and it sometimes will, users have the options to right-click on the e-mail and add it to a blocked-senders list, add it to a safe-senders list, which is useful when users find a legitimate e-mail in their junk mail folders, or add the sender's domain to a safe senders list, which is useful if the user does e-mail exchanges with many people from the same domain or business.

Suspected spam e-mails are sent to the junk mail folder in Outlook 2007. Users should review this periodically, especially when first setting up an account, to ensure no legitimate e-mail is being marked as spam.

There are other more advanced spam removal tools, such as dedicated hardware and server-based antispam software. Because both of these involve significant financial investment, and the goal of this book is to minimize financial impact while protecting computers and networks, this section only gives some recommendations for readers who want to conduct more research.

Barracuda is one of the more well-known and effective spam and virus firewalls. Their Web site can be found at **www.barra-**

cudanetworks.com. Barracuda provides hardware-based spam and virus firewall protection compared to most products that are software-based.

A 2009 report from Forrester Research found that 80 percent of enterprise customers used some version of Microsoft Office. In general, Office 2007 does a good job fighting spam. When used in conjunction with one of the antispam tools mentioned in this chapter, as well as in Chapter 11, it does an amazingly good job, as do most other e-mail applications with proven antispam software.

Microsoft SmartScreen is an intelligent spam-filtering solution that is built into Outlook 2007, the most recent version of this program, and Outlook 2003. This is the technology that Outlook uses to determine which e-mails are legitimate and which are spam. Additionally, it reviews embedded URLs in e-mails to check for potential phishing scams. Outlook 2007 also utilizes Outlook E-Mail Postmark, which helps analyze outgoing e-mails to prevent users from sending spam or bulk e-mail. Legitimate e-mails receive a "postmark," indicating they are valid. Inbound e-mail servers use this technology to verify the postmark and then the message is delivered to the inbox of the recipient.

The 10 Most Common E-mail Scams and How to Defend Against Them

E-mail scams are hoax e-mails that typically contain no harmful software, but instead request the user do something, such as send money. These messages take advantage of victims through grief, greed, or other methods to convince recipients to take a specific, desired action. Here are the ten most common e-mail scams or hoaxes from 2004-2009. Please note, although most of these seem like common sense things to avoid, these e-mail scams work and have defrauded many individuals out of their life savings.

1. Nigerian Prince

The first e-mail scam, which was the most widely used, is a variation of the Nigerian scam. In that e-mail, the author purports to be a Nigerian prince or man from a very wealthy family. Due to some unfortunate circumstances and legal hurdles, the sender asks victims to help him transfer a large sum of money and in return, the recipient can keep a large portion of the money. Recipients might be asked to pay for some legal fees, which the sender cannot because his accounts are currently frozen. This attack worked because many Americans know few rich Nigerian men and cannot validate whether the sender is who he says he is. The possibility of a large fee in return for a small investment catches people's attention and wallets. The attacker claims victims will get their money back within a few days. There seems to be no risk with a big payday.

Whenever someone asks for money through an e-mail, it is usually a scam. If they guarantee to send a huge payday in return for this help, it is a scam. The Nigerian e-mail scam has victimized thousands of people for millions of dollars. The latest variation of this scam is disguised as an e-mail from the Nigerian (or U.S.) government, looking to reimburse victims of the Nigerian scam. A person can claim up to $150,000 as a victim of the Nigerian scam as reimbursement for losses, as well as other damages. Of course, individuals must send some money to cover the legal fees to get the financial transactions completed. These individuals will never get the $150,000, and despite the fact that people lost millions in the Nigerian scam many more people sent money in to this scam, hoping to get some reimbursement from the original scam only to find out they were in fact scammed again.

2. Preapproved loans and credit cards

The second prevalent scam involves e-mails supposedly sent from reputable banks, which claim to offer recipients preapproved loans and credit cards; however, the recipient needs to pay a small fee before he or she can get the loan or credit card. Users can easily spot the fraud by paying attention to the details and of course using common sense and good security awareness. Banks and credit card companies might charge a fee, but only after people sign up with them, never in advance. As with any e-mail, users should never give out their credit card or bank account information to an unknown source.

3. Winning the lottery

The third e-mail scam is a lottery-related scam in which recipients are told they have won a big amount at the lottery or someone else won a large amount of money in the lottery and needs the recipient's help to move the money from his or her country into the recipient's country. Like the Nigerian scam, the sender needs some money in advance to complete the transfer and cover legal fees, in return for a very large payday. The money is so enticing that people might start dreaming about how to spend it and lose their common sense. The e-mail scam asks recipients to pay a small nominal processing fee to get the earnings or to give the sender access to the recipient's bank account so the scammer can move the lottery winnings into the user's possession temporarily.

4. Phishing e-mails

The fourth most common e-mail scam involves a wide variety of "phishing" e-mails in which users are directed to a Web site and asked to enter personal, financial, and other sensitive information. These might look like legitimate e-mails. Recipients can detect and counter them by never clicking on hyperlinks in e-mails and never entering personally identifiable or financial information or user names and passwords in Web sites that are not trusted. Users should double check the domain names of the Web sites to which they are directed and ensure they are the proper site, with the proper URL. The best advice to avoid phishing is to never click on an e-mail hyperlink and instead navigate directly to the Web site homepage in a new browser window by typing in the domain name or URL.

5. Responses to classified ads

In the fifth most common e-mail scam, attackers search for online classified ads victims have placed and offer them significantly more money than the asking price of the products the victim is selling. These requests are from overseas and claim the extra money will help the victim take care of international fees for them or move large sums of money out of the country. The scammers ask victims to deposit the difference between what they offer (in advance), minus a hefty commission for the victim. Once this is done, they will send the victim a money order or other fraudulent transfer document. After the victim sends the product, he or she finds out the transfer or money order was fraudulent, costing the victim both money and the product he or she was selling. Individuals should never transfer money to another account unless they are absolutely certain the online transaction is legitimate. One should never agree to take payments in excess of sale price to "move" money out of another country and never send someone money in advance of reimbursement from an unknown entity.

6. Job offers

The sixth most common hoax occurs when individuals post resumes or other personal contact information online or on Web sites. Someone will approach the poster and will want to hire him or her to deal with a complex financial transaction involving overseas accounts. The scammer will offer the victim a commission of the money he or she will handle. Then the scammer will ask the victim to provide personal information so the scammer can send the money to the victim directly. After the scammer gets the victim's information he or she either accesses the victim's bank accounts or steals his or her identity to withdraw money from the bank account or impersonate the victim through fraudulent credit card or other transactions.

7. Charity or donation opportunities

The seventh most popular e-mail hoaxes are the charity or donation hoaxes. These are very simple and highly effective because they appeal to the compassionate side of people. Some attackers abuse news of natural disasters or other tragic events to ask for money from the general public for a charity or cause. Before a person gives to any charitable organization, he or she should check to see if the people or companies asking for donations are legitimate and if they are associated with a legitimate relief association. Also, if users are asked to donate money to a certain cause via e-mail, it is probably a scam, because reputable organizations never ask for money via unsolicited e-mails. Those who really wish to donate to a worthy cause should do a quick search on the Internet to find a legitimate and well-known charitable organization. Users should not give money to anyone who sends them an unsolicited e-mail, no matter how convincing the e-mail might be.

8. Cheap vacations

The eighth most popular e-mail scam is the cheap vacation scam. Users get to take a vacation to a great resort for a very low price, but only if they agree to sign the deal in the next few hours through high-pressure sales techniques. After users sign the deal (usually without checking all the details) they will discover that there are extra fees (usually outrageous ones) or that the e-mail is completely fraudulent and they just gave away their credit card numbers or bank account access to criminals. Unbelievable deals that seem too good to be true probably are. Scammers are just trying to lure victims into releasing their financial account information or credit card data. Users should make sure to read all the fine print and thoroughly review contracts before signing them. Companies and individuals want e-mail users to sign up for limited time offers so they feel they do not have enough time to look over the agreement without the risk of missing out on the amazing deal. Also any unsolicited e-mail that offers great deals is probably a scam.

9. Pyramid scheme

Ninth in popularity are the pyramid scheme e-mail scams. Scammers send victims a get-rich-quick scheme that is easy for the average Joe to use. All the recipients have to do is send in a small amount of money to get started. Then they are instructed to send the e-mail to their friends, family, and other contacts and get them to do the same thing. As the recipient's network grows, in theory so do his or her profits. The promise is that if recipients send money, they will be added to the growing list of people and will eventually earn plenty of money for doing nothing. The problem with it, besides wasting people's time and money, is that recipients are participating in a pyramid scam, which is illegal, and recipients can be indicted for fraud. The scheme is constructed so that one person will be at the top of the list and will get the bulk of the money; this person is not the recipient of these e-mails.

If someone e-mails about a quick and easy way to make money, it is probably a scam. If e-mails ask recipients to send money, it is a scam. If they ask recipients to get more people to participate in the deal, it is definitely an e-mail scam. The first person on the list makes the bulk of the money and the people below him or her make less (or none). Each person below the first person brings in more people, who bring more people, etc. Soon enough there are thousands of people participating in the scam. The more people there are and the lower down the list they are situated, the less money recipients will gain from the scheme. In fact, in most cases, recipients simply lose money, energy, and time.

10. Home-based business opportunity

And finally, the tenth most popular e-mail scam offers recipients money for a home-based, online business or other Internet work scam in which individuals do very little for a very high income. Quotes from "real" people who became rich are usually associated with this scam. The money is said to be good and the work is easy. People fall for this one because easy money sounds good. Of course, recipients do have to "invest" a few hundred dollars or so to get the software, books, or other starter items. Individuals just need to supply the sender with their bank account, credit card, or PayPal account information so they can be charged for these starter supplies. In turn, the scammers either steal victims' money using their personal data, or they give victims a starter kit to a business venture that will never generate any revenue, making the transaction a legitimate business sale that resulted in victims buying worthless products. Typically, the type of work involves clicking on Google AdWords advertisements, which generates revenue on a pay-per-click basis for someone else. This is also illegal. Victims soon find out they have earned little to nothing for their efforts. Often, to access the "earnings," users must pay an additional transaction fee of around $50, only to find out they have earned little or no money, so they are out their initial investment and the transaction fee.

Combating spam, spoofing, phishing, and hoaxes is not difficult. Good antispam software, good antivirus software, and a large amount of common sense and security awareness will keep users from being victimized by these threats.

CASE STUDY: FEEDING OFF SPAM WITH VIRCOM'S modusGATE™

Vircom, Inc.
www.vircom.com
1-888-484-7266

Equipatan, established in 1968, was the first Canadian company to distribute industrial products through a catalog. Today, it remains a leader on the industrial marketplace through phone, fax, online, and retail store sales, with more than 450,000 products available.

The Challenge

Equipatan, a Canadian online vendor and retailer of industrial products, was being inundated with email messages. Unfortunately, the messages were not customer orders but automated return-to-sender notices. Curiously, the return-to-sender messages were not a by-product of mail originating from the company.

"These e-mail messages started to arrive in the hundreds, then in the thousands," explained McGregor the Network Administrator for Equipatan. "In a very short period of time, we had received well over a million e-mails, clogging our mail servers and threatening to shut us down completely. For an organization that is as heavily dependent upon e-mail as we are, this threat could be devastating to all of the company's operations."

The Attack

Equipatan was inundated with e-mail because of a Joe-job, something that has become more prevalent in the e-mail world. A Joe-job is a spam attack that uses a spoofed or forged sender address, often as an act of revenge. Joe-job attacks result in non-delivery reports, out-of-office notices, challenge-responses, auto-responders, etc., which are generated with the forged sender address. The barrage of spam can often sully the sender's reputation and incur the wrath of the unfortunate recipients.

The mail server receiving these spam messages bounce them back to the unsuspecting sender. When copious amounts of e-mail messages are bounced, the organization's domain name and/or IP address risks being blacklisted — a list of domain names and IP addresses that are reportedly being abused — as a source for spam. The influx of e-mail may also cause the organization's e-mail server to process e-mail too slowly or even shut down.

For the company, this particular Joe-job resulted in a flood of bounced e-mail messages, most of which were sent to random and non-existent addresses on their domain. This attack was damaging because the company's e-mail gateway was incapable of handling the increased load.

"The load of bounced-back e-mail messages was so great that our existing e-mail gateway and server just couldn't handle it. Messages were piling up exponentially. And to make it worse, we couldn't get any legitimate e-mails either in or out," said McGregor. McGregor and his team at Equipatan had to make an important decision and they had to make it quickly.

The Decision

"We realized there were two ways to go: either we could just wait out this storm, which we knew would not be viable, or we could get additional assistance," McGregor continued. "If we were going to remain operational, then we knew we had to get help quickly."

McGregor's group contacted a number of antispam developers before they came upon a Canadian-based computer reseller and integrator. Equipatan was recommended to contact Vircom, for who they were a reseller for their modusGate™ secure e-mail gateway solutions.

Shortly after their initial contact, Vircom's SpamBuster Team remotely accessed the company's e-mail servers, which were in the midst of another malicious Joe-job attack. The SpamBuster Team quickly identified the problem and recommended a solution. "What they found was that the majority of the e-mail messages were coming from randomly chosen names combined with the company's domain name; for example, 'randomname1@equipatan.com'," explained Mike Petsalis, COO for Vircom

With little time to spare before the e-mail infrastructure collapsed, two Vircom support technicians arrived at Equipatan's headquarters to install and configure a 500-user modusGate™ Appliance, incorporating Norman Anti-Virus. The modusGate™ Appliance is designed to verify all local e-mail addresses before accepting inbound messages. If the recipients are valid, messages are scanned and processed according to the mail content settings. Messages to non-valid addresses are normally returned to the sending server but, in this case, a temporary custom script was created to quarantine the bounced messages.

"Although it is usually against RFC recommendations to discard bounced-back messages," said Petsalis, "in this case, we really did not have a choice.

Either we violate the RFC recommendations for a short period so that they become operational again or we maintain RFC 'purity' and they stay down. In this case, we chose the first option."

The Result

By the end of the day, the company's e-mail infrastructure was back online and e-mail traffic was flowing. McGregor also took advantage of modusGate's™ Web interface to remotely monitor the e-mail traffic while he was on a business trip that evening.

The cost for this fix was just under $8,000 CAN. Its worth to the company, however, was priceless. "With minimal losses in terms of productivity, we were able to keep external incoming/outgoing e-mail running," MacGregor said. The company's return on investment was immediate. Similarly, maintenance costs are minimal thanks to modusGate's™ Appliance "set-it-and-forget-it" functions. By thinking long-term and allocating the appropriate funds for the modusGate™ Appliance at the time of the attack, Equipatan has not needed to purchase product enhancements to fix gaps that likely would have likely arisen had another solution been chosen. And, as a Vircom client, the company reaps the benefits of continual enhancements to the modus suite of products.

Today, electronic mail is crucial to any business wanting to be both competitive and successful. In most cases, it forms the backbone of an organization's day-to-day activities and its uses will certainly continue to evolve. Therefore, organizations will always need protection from the potentially harmful elements of e-mail, such as spam and viruses, and the perpetrators of malicious attacks such as Joe-jobs.

About Vircom

*Vircom, Inc., based in Montreal, is a privately held software development and professional services company focused exclusively on e-mail messaging security. Founded in 1994, Vircom is the only e-mail security vendor to offer a wide range of deployment options, proprietary antispam technology, complete Windows™ infrastructure integration, and premium customer service. Its award-winning products include modusMail™, modusGate™, modusGate™ Appliance. Vircom technology is made available to several major security providers and deployed through third-party vendors to customers in more than 100 countries. For additional information, please visit **www.vircom.com** or call 1-888-484-7266.*

About EmailSecurityMatters.com

*EmailSecurityMatters.com is a community portal where users and experts exchange security news and tips, best practices, and discuss and analyze new e-mail security technologies. For additional information, please visit **www.emailsecuritymatters.com.***

CHAPTER 5

Detecting and Countering Malware & Spyware

This chapter is dedicated to understanding, detecting, preventing, and eliminating malware and spyware. Malware comes from the combination of the words "malicious" and "software." The software is used for malicious intentions that are typically illegal, depending on the laws in the software victim's country. Malware attempts to infiltrate a user's personal computer and/or network, and either collect data, steal money, take over that person's computer, or a combination of these actions. It also sometimes is designed to damage or destroy computer files, operating systems, and computer data, as well as disrupt services, capability, or operations of a computer, network, or entire business. Malware is intentionally sneaky by design and tries to remain hidden in users' computers.

Malware can come in a variety of forms based on its design and intent. Although typically it is installed or downloaded from Web sites, through e-mail, or as part of another software installation, malware can sometimes copy itself to various parts in a user's personal computer and be distributed across the Internet, spreading the infection. The more computers infected with a particular malware, the more data is compromised and the more opportunity the program has to inflict damage and achieve illegal financial gain. Malware must spread to be effective. Malware designers distribute their software widely, hoping for a significant impact upon payload delivery and infection.

Spyware is a combination of the words "spying" and "software," and, like its name suggests, it is software that hides in a user's personal computer or network with the intent of collecting personal information, primarily for illicit financial gain. Spyware is malware, but it has a very specific purpose. Spyware comes in many forms, such as a Trojan horse, which appears to be perfectly legitimate software but has code secretly embedded into it, unknown to the user, which begins to perform its functions when activated. Like the great horse in the city of Troy, this Trojan horse also houses dangers inside of it. In most cases, without advanced detection software, users will never notice their computers have been infiltrated and infected. Spyware is very powerful, because it can cause financial damage or destruction to a user, a user's business, personal finances, and more. Adware or malware might only destroy the operating system or specific data on the system. It can take years to restore the damage from spyware, if ever.

Both spyware and malware are malicious pieces of software that cause damage to the infected computer or network. The programs spread in various ways, which include exploiting software and operating system bugs and security holes, getting in through open ports, and tricking the user through e-mail attachments. An open port is a TCP/IP port number that is configured to accept packets. Open ports can be exploited. Ports can be closed, in which case they will deny all packets or network traffic. TCP/IP is the communication protocol for the Internet. Most traffic on the Internet, including Web browsing and e-mail, uses the TCP/IP protocol. To communicate and transmit packets of information, certain ports must be open on Web servers and exchange servers. For example, HTTP uses port 80 and HTTPS uses port 443.

The main problem with spyware and malware is that they are usually hard to detect. Although there are tools to deal with the programs, they are not always 100 percent effective. Another problem is the amount of malware and spyware roaming the Internet. Malware developers embed their software within otherwise-reputable software, which the user would presume to be perfectly safe to download and execute. Often, malware programs take the source code of the legitimate product and modify it, or they take the actual compiled software and modify it by adding the malware right into the installation procedure, making it nearly impossible to discover without antispyware software. Of course, the malware does more than just damage a user's computer in these cases; it can severely damage the reputation of the these legitimate software manufacturers.

Spyware can detect users' keystrokes, steal passwords, copy critical files, steal financial and other data, intercept e-mails, and more. It can expose all of a user's online accounts to illegal access and cause severe disruption to both home and business finances. Unfortunately, coders create malicious software for fun; for practice; and to test the security of computers, networks, and operating systems to see if they can access private data.

There are ways in which a user can discover whether a personal computer is infested with spyware and/or malware and there are ways to remove them. A computer user's first defense is antivirus software. Many Internet security suites and modern antivirus software applications have built-in antimalware protection of varying degrees of effectiveness. There is also software specifically designed to combat malware and spyware.

As with antivirus software, antimalware and antispyware must be updated routinely. Malicious coders have the advantage; they can create malware and release it out into the Internet. After the program is detected, antimalware companies must create solutions to detect and remove it. Just like viruses, malware can be mutated into new versions, which might or might not be detected by antimalware software; therefore, regularly updating antimalware will ensure a computer is best protected against infection. Most malware and spyware is spread without the computer user's knowledge, consent, or intent. Many people have no antimalware protection, no firewalls, no (or out of date) antivirus software, and do not install the latest patches for their operating system. They are defenseless against malware and are unwilling participants in propagating it throughout their network and Internet. Depending on which antimalware protection you use, you may have to manually update it. The good news is that most modern antimalware applications automatically update their definitions on a routine basis. You should review your antivirus software and antimalware to schedule automatic updates.

Besides antivirus programs, it is advisable to have strong firewall software, in addition to hardware firewalls such as routers, which block both inbound and outbound connections. There are various types of malware, which are categorized depending on what the programs do, how they do it, and what they ultimately are designed to achieve. There are viruses, worms, rootkits, Trojan horses, SQL injections, spyware, adware, crimeware, and more. The following pages offer a look at some of the wide variety of malware on the Internet.

Viruses

A virus is a variety of malware that infects various types of operating systems and platforms, even some cell phones. After infection, viruses spread themselves into many of the different files in the operating system so they will be harder to remove. The virus finds new people to infect through built-in functionality or accessing e-mail address books or contact lists. It spam e-mails all of a user's listed friends, family members, and business associates. Some viruses are coded to execute on a certain date and time, often months in the future, and some simply destroy a PC's operating system and data files. The best defense against viruses is up-to-date antivirus software.

Worms

Worms are malicious software products whose primarily purpose is to replicate themselves and activate a malware or spyware attack. The replication technology, or the ability to copy itself again and again with each copy repeating the process of copying and spreading, is oftentimes used in viruses as well and can be very difficult to eradicate. Worms can copy themselves inside the contents of many other folders or files on a computer, including operating system files. A worm typically copies itself to a piece of data in a file that the user does not normally see, often by replacing the data file, so it is difficult to detect. Worms can defend against detection by replicating in hidden folders and files and mimicking valid system files. Worms can bore down into operating-system and other software application folders, affecting their ability to launch or perform normally.

The goal of a worm is to keep a computer infected until the attacker activates it to destroy data, take over functions of a computer, or activate spyware. As with most spyware, a worm is primarily used for illicit financial gain or to launch distributed denial of service attacks. A distributed denial of service attack is an attack in which many computers all over the world communicate with one Web site or Web browser simultaneously, consuming bandwidth and crippling the server's functionality, rendering it unavailable for its intended purpose. Denial of service attacks can bring a large business or government Web site to its knees.

Worms usually (but not always) have minimal actual effect on the computer system they infect, because their primary purpose is to spread infection to other computers and networks. Worms will consume bandwidth in disk space and memory space. Their major damage comes from the propagation of the worm itself through the infection of other computers. Because worms both abuse security holes and have the ability to infect multiple files, they are very efficient and might be present in various Web sites and e-mail attachments throughout the world, spreading across the Internet with impressive speed. Worms can either be designed for destruction of data or as spyware for theft of user names, passwords, and financial data. As mentioned earlier, a worm can act as a "mule," carrying a malware payload that will cause damage at a later time when activated; therefore, worm detection and removal is critical. Worms have been used for extortion, after the theft of personal and financial information. Worms can also be used as spyware to collect information, user names, passwords, and keystrokes and transmit that information to the attacker.

Worms can also be used to install "backdoors" into a computer. A backdoor is an opening created through the firewall and other security protection measures that allows an attacker to access the computer or network undetected. It can also be used to turn a PC into a botnet, a computer that is part of a large network of PCs taken over by hackers to perform denial of service attacks. Some worms can affect a computer's resources by consuming central processing unit (CPU) resources and hogging memory, affecting computer performance negatively. Most antivirus security suites and antimalware can detect and remove worms. Users should make sure they scan external devices, such as portable hard drives, flash drives, and other portable media, for worms as well. Users should ensure they have updated antivirus software and antimalware running at all times and use a solid firewall to block worm attacks.

Trojan Horse

A Trojan horse is malware that disguises itself as a genuine and beneficial piece of software, but performs unintended actions on a system by releasing malware or spyware on the infected computer. This malware got its name from the legendary Trojan War. The Greeks left a large wooden horse as a gift outside of the gates of Troy (the city of their enemies the Trojans). The Greeks hid soldiers in the horse, and when the Trojans took it into the city of their own volition, the soldiers sprung out of it and conquered the otherwise well-guarded city. A Trojan horse exploits the user as the hole in the computer system's defenses, rather than bugs and operating-system security holes, which are regularly fixed and patched by the manufacturer. The user is the weakest part of a computer system, and if the user has certain software, especially freeware, or free software, obtained on the Internet, he or she might be unintentionally installing Trojans into the system. By design, a Trojan horse does not get instant access to all of the computer's resources, as it is typically limited by user privileges. If it infects a restricted user, it has limited resources and abilities to inflict damage; however, many Trojan horses are specifically created to exploit bugs and holes in software and operating systems, enabling it to have much more destructive power.

A Trojan horse is used for various activities, such as uninstalling programs, installing spyware, keyloggers, and other malicious software. A Trojan horse can also install other malware programs, such as viruses and rootkits, send data files to the attacker, place files onto the computer or network, and enable unauthorized access and data storage. Trojan horses have been used to store illegal, copyrighted, or pornographic material on computers or establish unauthorized file transfer protocol (FTP) sessions for illegal download and distribution. FTP is a network protocol used primarily to transfer files over the Internet. A Trojan horse can also be used to establish Web servers, game servers, and FTP servers on computers or networks without users' knowledge, consuming a computer's resources and bandwidth, while creating access points for illegal activities.

Trojan horses can also allow the attacker to view the screen of the infected computer, as well as pull "pranks" on the infected PC, such as changing screen resolution or screen savers, rebooting the PC, and remotely controlling the mouse cursor. A Trojan horse infection causes a wide-open backdoor that stays on a computer system for a long time, allowing even more attackers to gain access to the computer without a user's knowledge. Trojan horses are used to either gain money by making the computer system a part of a botnet and sending e-mail spam from it, for a distributed denial of service attack, or to gain personal information that is sometimes used to destroy a person or a company through financial or corporate data theft or extortion.

Trojan horses distribute themselves in different software products that appear to be perfectly safe to the average user. The attacker makes sure the original functionality of these applications is not affected and that the Trojan horse is installed discretely, without detection. In many cases, this software, which is typically freeware or shareware — software that is typically given away at no cost, but often with limited functionality until a full license is purchased — gets rave reviews and others download it, creating an ever-growing list of infected computers and networks.

Trojan horses are delivered via Web site downloads in the form of executable content, such as an ActiveX control or other software download, and some are embedded into spam e-mail attachments with enticing incentives to open the attachment. ActiveX controls are add-on programs to Web browsers. They are used to enhance your browsing experience or add in third-party software functionality, such as Microsoft Update. Some Trojans actively search the Internet for computers that have certain security holes or have not been properly patched and exploit these known security weaknesses. Besides carefully checking the reputation of online Web sites and product downloads, users should have active antivirus and antimalware programs installed and updated at all times.

Users should not allow Web sites to spontaneously launch and run JavaScript, Java, Flash, or ActiveX products, which are used regularly to implant Trojan horses and other malware on computer systems. Web browser settings should be set so as to require users' confirmation to activate those software products.

Rootkits

A rootkit is malware that allows the attacker to infiltrate a computer and achieve unlimited control over it. The rootkit is designed to hide itself deep within the computer system where the user will not be able to detect it and it is extremely difficult to remove. Rootkits allow an attacker complete control over a user's system — unlike a Trojan horse, which only gives the attacker as much freedom as the infected user has. Rootkits can get deep inside computer systems, in places that even users do not have access to, because these places contain important files and executables for the operating system. A rootkit essentially becomes a part of the operating system and gets more access and privileges than even system administrators. A rootkit can evade detection from antivirus products and other antimalware products, making it look like a computer is safe and uninfected.

Some rootkits arrive as a Trojan horse. In one famous case, a music company inserted rootkits into its CDs to achieve more control over them, which resulted in many computer problems for the users who bought them. Rootkits can also open backdoors into a system and make it much more vulnerable to a malicious software attack. Unlike viruses, which are usually built to exploit one specific operating system and targeted to specific security holes, rootkits are available for a wide variety of operating systems and, because they offer complete control and concealment, they are much more dangerous. The term rootkit came from the Linux and UNIX operating systems in which the highest user, the user who has no limits, is called a root user. In some other operating systems, this is called the administrator account.

Rootkits are used for both good and malicious intentions. A rootkit can be a single program that offers complete control of an infected computer and can also bind with other software products installed on a PC. Because rootkits are so smart and well-designed, they are hard to discover and a specific rootkit detector is needed, together with a deep probe into the computer system, to check if it is compromised or infected. Some antimalware programs also use signatures to detect known rootkit software — both legal and illegal. Rootkits have also been used to hide other malware programs such as viruses and spyware. Ready-to-compile code for simple rootkits is available all over the Internet, which helps spread rootkits even further. But, rootkits can also be used for good purposes, such as in an antivirus program that needs to be buried deeply into the operating system to protect against viruses and other hacking attempts.

A firmware rootkit is one that has been compiled into a firmware or hardware upgrade to ensure perpetual reinfection of the host computer. Because firmware or hardware is built into the computer, reinfection happens over and over again until the firmware is replaced and/or overwritten with proper coding. This rootkit uses a firmware vulnerability: the failure to perform code integrity checks to ensure the original firmware code has not been modified. This simple fact leaves it open for attacks by rootkit writers. There have been widely publicized cases that illustrate firmware rootkits. In Europe, rootkits tampered with credit card readers, leading to stolen credit card data and ultimately causing significant financial damage.

It is also possible to implement a rootkit into a computer's basic input/basic output system (BIOS). BIOS is a piece of software that determines the basic hardware properties of a computer system. Another rootkit is the one in the hypervisor level. A hypervisor is a piece of software or hardware that allows a computer to run several operating systems at the same time. The rootkit will run the user's operating system on a virtual machine, a piece of software that simulates the hardware the operating system requires to operate. A virtual machine can run the operating system as if the software does not exist, allowing the rootkit to intercept and modify any data the user sends to it and any data the computer sends back. There is a free software product from Microsoft called Rootkit Revealer, which is made to help users detect and protect against generic versions of these rootkit types. This software is available for free at **http://technet.microsoft.com/en-us/sysinternals/bb897445.aspx**. However, rootkits are very hard to combat.

Another version of a rootkit is the bootloader rootkit, which is also known as a bootkit and an "Evil Maid attack." This type of rootkit places itself in the bootloader, which loads the operating system when a computer is turned on. This rootkit can bypass encryption by being there to record the data when the computer decrypts it. This attack is also hard to combat; users need to have a trusted module made and its entire job will be to protect the boot-path, which will disallow the rootkit to load itself before loading the operating system. The boot-path is the location of the boot.ini file, which determines which operating system options to display when the Startup program is running in a Windows-based computer.

There is also a kernel rootkit that replaces or adds its code to the operating-system kernel and the device drivers of the system. The kernel is the core of the operating system. Device drivers are a way for the operating system to communicate with the computer system's hardware products. Some operating systems allow device drivers to operate with the same privileges the operating system enjoys and because of this, the kernal rootkits gain plenty of free reign to do whatever they desire. If a rootkit penetrates the kernel, either in the form of a device driver or a kernel module, it is considered very dangerous because it has attained a deep level of concealment and control over the computer. In many cases, the only way to recover from a rootkit is a complete reformatting of the hard drive and reinstallation of the operating system. There is also a library-level rootkit, which operates by patching or re-placing system calls. System calls are a way for an application to request a certain resource from the operating system. Those resources are disk space, memory space, and so on.

One way to stop a rootkit that has infected a computer is to check the validity of system file, known as .DLLs or code libraries, against the original files. A dynamic-link library (DLL) is an ex-ecutable file that acts as a shared library of functions. Users can check to see if these files have been changed in any way (size, date, contents, etc.). Digital signatures can also be used to detect infected .DLL files. A digital signature is an electronic signature used to authenticate that the original content of the message or file is unchanged and authentic. Digital signatures basically encrypt a file using a mathematical formula and the result is the signature. A program that uses digital signatures checks if the file produces the same result as before if it is put through the same mathematical formula. If not, it is compromised.

There are also rootkits in the application level, which replace certain applications with Trojan horses that masquerade as those programs so the user will not notice that something is wrong. They also use patches to change normal software products and turn them into rootkit software products. Rootkits are tough to detect and harder to remove. Some rootkits can be detected using signatures, while others might be detected using a heuristic-based method. The best defense against rootkits is updated antimalware protection that specifically states it can detect and remove rootkits.

Adware

Adware is a type of software, distributed for free, that relies on constantly updating its data, because its developers get their income through residual income from advertisements the software displays. This method has been used in saturated markets, such as through instant messengers, where users have the use of free software in exchange for advertisement space on their computer screens. Often, new computers come loaded with various types of adware programs. Typically, in exchange for the use of free software, Web sites, discussion boards, and other applications, ad space is sold and displayed as compensation for the use of these free applications. The ads are usually consistent in size, can be static or dynamic, and rotate on a fixed interval. They are embedded with hyperlinks to other Web sites. Clicks on the advertisement might generate residual income, affiliate sales commissions, and more for the software or Web site provider. Some of these ads are minimal in size and impact, but some use enormous bandwidth, are very intrusive, and are hard to eradicate.

Although adware is usually not considered to be malware by technical definition, some adware can be used as spyware, because it can collect data about the user, typically in the form of purchases, Internet activity, and interests. This data is used to determine which advertisement are served and displayed. By targeting users with products in fields they are interested in, there is a greater chance of sales conversions. Because the ads are constantly updated, the adware takes a constant toll on the user's bandwidth and might slow down other programs while accessing the Internet. They are also a nuisance, because some ads feature moving images or take up a considerable amount of screen space. Adware often takes the form of a toolbar for a Web browser or as an instant messenger program. They are easily detected and removed by most Internet security suites, as well as antimalware and anti-adware applications. In general, adware programs are not malicious and, though annoying, are usually harmless.

Crimeware

Crimeware is software written specifically to automate the process of cyber crime and is typically used to steal financial data and personally identifiable information for use in illicit, unlawful activities for the creator's financial gain. Crimeware can install keystroke loggers on a computer to collect sensitive information as it is typed by the user. Every single key pressed is recorded, saved, and transmitted back to the attacker. Crimeware can also automate phishing attacks in which a user enters a URL of a Web site he or she wants to visit on a Web browser and is redirected to a similar-looking Web site where the user's personal data might be stolen. Crimeware can also be used to steal computer or Web site passwords, because the computer can wait for a user to enter a certain personal account.

Crimeware might allow the attacker access to the infected machine remotely. Crimeware usually infects computers via backdoors, holes in Web applications, or through e-mail attachments with the assistance of social engineering. Crimeware also spreads by searching for certain open ports in various computer systems and by using them to install the software remotely on the computer. A port, used on TCP/IP networks to transfer files, is a way for one software program in one computer to communicate with software in another computer. Crimeware is malware and often spyware, and it is fought through traditional means as well as through regulation and laws that strictly forbid its use.

Grayware

Besides malware and spyware, there is also grayware. Grayware is a general term used to classify software products that are not considered malware, but are still annoying or perform undesirable means, such as annoying Web page pop-ups, tracking Internet user browsing activity, or allowing other computer vulnerabilities. Its effects are less serious than malware's effects, but these programs can still negatively impact a computer. Grayware encompasses some of the spyware and adware products previously discussed, as well as dialers, prank or joke products, and tools for remote access.

Denial of Service Attack

An attacker uses a denial of service (DoS) attack to use up a computer's resources through the use of another computer or a software product, causing the computer to be unavailable to other, legitimate users. The attack is usually done via computer software that performs actions such as automatically requesting multiple Web pages from the victim computer, which is usually a server. Because the server thinks the attack is a human user, it sends the Web pages, getting clogged up due to the processing power and bandwidth that its actions consume.

Denial of service attacks became outdated several years ago when servers and computers became more advanced and had more powerful resources; they have too much memory and bandwidth for one computer to effectively impair. Additionally, if a computer starts using too many resources, it can easily be tracked by the administrators of that Web site or Web server through the assigned IP address and be removed from the network or have the Web site and Web server permanently shut down. Because it is so easy today to track an IP address to an ISP and report that IP address for abuse, a traditional denial of service attack is no longer effective.

Because of this, a more advanced Distributed Denial of Service (DDoS) attack started appearing. A DDoS attack subverts the attempts to trace and stop the abusing computer by using hundreds to tens of thousands of computers and IPs to perform the malicious attack. The volume of computers participating in a DDoS attack can render Web sites and Web servers unavailable. Coordinating such a massive attack with other uses is practically impossible, so botnets or other malware are used to control the resources of other computers, without the owners' knowledge, to perform the DDoS attacks. A DDoS attack either makes the Web site or resource unavailable to other users or makes it load so slowly that users get impatient and move on to a different Web site altogether.

In denial of service, there are two types of attacks: the wired attack and the wireless attack. To attack wired networks requires plenty of computing power and sometimes a distributed form of the denial of service attack. In this type, attackers must create software to create bots (individual computers the hacker controls), which in unison create the botnet (a network of bots). Attackers who target wired networks need to use computers that have broadband connections that will handle all the traffic going to the target computers and the traffic they will output, as well. The more Web traffic each computer can receive and send, the more powerful the DDoS attack. Attacking wireless networks is accomplished the same way, except that these attacks target wireless network signals, which are usually much easier to overload.

Users can recognize a denial of service attack by checking their servers' performance logs. They might also experience very slow networking, Web site unavailability, inability to connect to the network, failed wireless connections, or other communication failures. Users can also notice a denial of service attack if they see a dramatic rise in the amount of spam e-mails they receive in their e-mail inboxes. In this case, users might experience what is referred to as an e-mail bomb. In an e-mail bomb, a huge amount of e-mail is sent to a company's e-mail addresses in an attempt to overload and crash the servers. Users might also want to check their routers to see if there is a large increase in the amount of strain on the network's bandwidth.

Robots

Computers infected with a malicious software product intended to be used to control their systems are called zombie computers. They can also be part of a botnet, a network of "robots." They are nicknamed robots because they do whatever the attacker says automatically, just like robots. Attackers hide malicious software inside a normal software product an average user would employ, such as instant messengers or games. As discussed previously, Webbots, or bots for short, can be used in distributed denial of service attacks. Most modern antimalware products will detect and remove this form of malware.

SQL Injection Attack

According to IBM's X-Force, there were more than one million SQL injection or SQL insertion attacks a day in 2009. Structured Query Language (SQL) is computer language used to mange data contained in relational databases. This attack will only affect computers or servers running SQL-based databases or SQL-server software. An SQL Server is a Web-based software designed to Web-enable SQL databases and create database powered applications. In this attack, malicious code is inserted into strings that are then passed to and executed by the SQL server. This technique "injects" malicious code by exploiting vulnerabilities in the database layer of a Web application. The generated SQL code is altered and ultimately executed on the Web server, giving hackers the ability to steal data and gain access to data in a user's database.

Any time a user enters data onto a Web form, makes purchases online, or uses online applications, he or she normally is accessing a database. Databases can hold customer data, transaction histories, financial data, bank account information, credit card records, personal information, health records, and corporate data. SQL injection attacks allow hackers access to view, alter, or destroy critical database files. The good news is this is a Web site server vulnerability, not a personal computer vulnerability, and can only affect a personal computer user if he or she has a Web site running SQL. Those who operate Web servers or Web sites need to ensure they have security measures in place to prevent SQL injection. There is an enormous amount of information on the Web and from Microsoft on how to secure databases against the threat of SQL injection attacks.

Cross-Site Scripting (XSS)

Cross-site scripting, or XSS for short, is another type of an injection attack. In this attack, malicious scripts are inserted into a Web site's basic HTML code. The attacker then uses a Web application to send malicious code through a client-side script, which is embedded in the Web page code and executed when the page is loaded in a Web browser, meaning it affects the version of the Web site the visitor sees. An Internet user's browser will run scripts on nearly every Web site the user encounters; therefore, malicious scripts can be quite damaging. These exploits can affect JavaScript, VBScript, Flash, HTML, and other client-side scripting languages. Users can disable scripts from running in a browser, but by default, they do run from trusted Web sites. Because users have no idea an XSS script is malicious and might be on an otherwise trusted site, most users will not block the script from being read and executed in their browsers.

The primary intent of XSS is to steal personal data from the site visitor and modify the structure of the Web sites it infects. A typical use of XSS is that it is injected into Web sites that use shopping cart software. The XSS scripts will execute when the browser is loaded on the site and the user is quickly redirected to a fraudulent, but authentic-looking Web site. This lets the attacker steal personal information and credit card data.

Cross-Site Forgery Request

Cross-Site Request Forgery (CSRF) is similar to cross-site scripting in that the user navigates to a legitimate Web page that has malicious scripting code inserted into it. The code executes when the page is loaded in the browser. In this attack, the "cookie" or "session ID" — a unique number that a Web server assigns to a user during a specific Web site visit for identification and tracking purposes — is hijacked by the attacker and the Web site believes that the attacker is the authenticated user, giving the attacker access to personal information, including credit card and other information, stored on the Web site. This lets the attacker place orders with the victim's credit card, change an account password, change an account address, and change an account e-mail address.

You can prevent this type of attack by blocking session cookies and disabling scripting in the browser; however, this also limits functionality and typically prevents users from completing online e-commerce transactions. To block session cookies in Internet Explorer, click on Tools, then Internet Options, then the Privacy Tab, and click "Override automatic cookie handling." You can specify exactly how you want Internet Explorer to handle cookies. To disable scripting in Internet Explorer, click on Tools, then Internet Options, and then the Security tab. Choose the zone you wish to modify, and click the "custom level" button. In this menu, you can turn off scripting, Active-X and many other Web site add-ons. Please note that you might reduce significant functionality in many Web sites if you turn off these features.

Relay Attack

In a relay attack, a perpetrator sends a message disguised as someone from whom the recipient is used to getting messages. The recipient can be either human or machine. The person whose identity the attacker uses is sometimes unaware of the attack. A relay attack is a form of the "man-in-the-middle" attack in which someone steps into a "conversation" between two computers and intercepts the transmission. This intercepted transmission can then be read, altered, and replaced with a new transmission from the hacker, exposing sensitive data to the hacker and allowing installation of malware onto the computer. A relay attack is primarily used to compromise and steal financial and other personal data for malicious use or fraud.

Here is a quick look at some of the other variety of malware in existence today:

- **Man-in-the-middle attacks**: This type of attack is quite effective. With improper security settings in browsers and Web sites that mix secure and nonsecure content on the same page, hackers can bypass secure socket layer (SSL) encryption, which provides secure communications over networks, including the Internet. The attackers also can intercept data by directing Internet users to the Web site via a proxy server, which is a server on the Internet that acts as an intermediary between the requesting client and the destination server. The key here is that users are actually going to be directed to the real site they intended to transact with; however, it is done via a proxy server — the middle man. Legitimate traffic is intercepted and either forged by the hacker or simply intercepted and read. By using a proxy server, the hacker can easily steal credit card and financial account login data quickly by monitoring a user's Web communications and stealing data as it is passed.

Simple ways users can prevent this in a secure session are to ensure that they have the LOCK icon displayed in their browser session window and are in a secure Web session. To ensure a URL is an authentic domain, users should make sure it displays the https:// versus just the http://. They can also review the SSL certificate credentials by clicking on the SSL LOCK icon in the browser window. On a non-secure site, this attack is even trickier to detect and might be completely invisible to a user. Because these attacks are almost always delivered via an e-mail asking recipients to log into their accounts, the best way to avoid this is to never click on links in an e-mail. If users need to log into an account they should simply open a new browser window and type in the URL.

- **Context-aware phishing and spear phishing**: Context-aware phishing, also known as spear phishing, is a targeted phishing scam. Instead of bulk e-mail delivery to thousands of e-mail addresses, it is more selective and targets affiliations or associations individuals might have with businesses or other entities. How many e-mails have you gotten from a bank you have never heard of and do not have an account with asking you to log in and change your password? This is an example of a nontargeted phishing campaign. Attackers send out a million e-mails, hoping a percentage of people actually use this bank and an even smaller percentage fall for the scam. If that e-mail came from, or appeared to come from, the recipient's credit union, he or she might take notice of it and actually "consider" the content of the e-mail. This e-mail has a much higher chance of actually being successful. Context-aware attacks are prominent on social networking sites. Modern antimalware programs can help protect against phishing Web sites, but nothing takes the place of common sense and good Web security habits.

- **Bank Trojans**: Bank Trojans are a fairly new and nasty Trojan designed to obtain access to online bank accounts. Bank Trojans are spread through e-mails, but can also be installed by visiting malicious Web sites or through other normal means of distributing malware. Bank Trojans are malware programs that reside on a computer in a dormant, normally undetectable state. When users access an online bank account, the trojans activate, steal the user names, passwords, security authentication answers, and even log keystrokes. This information is then used to access the user's accounts and remove funds. More advanced Bank Trojans use man-in-the-middle techniques to execute fund transfers automatically during sessions and also direct users to fraudulent Web sites displaying the balances before attackers cleaned out the account so users have no knowledge their finances were just stolen.

The key to defending against all malware and spyware is to use common sense and good Web security habits. Some examples are:

- Do not respond to unsolicited e-mails.

- Do not click on hyperlinks in e-mails.

- Do not download or install software unless it is from a trusted source.

- Do not install applets, browser plug-ins, etc.

- Do type in the URL of Web sites in a new browser window instead of clicking on links on Web pages or in e-mails.

- Do have a current antivirus, security suite, antimalware, and other active protection software installed and updated.

- Do ensure all operating-system and other software updates and patches are installed routinely.

CASE STUDY: THE COST OF SPYWARE TO YOUR BUSINESS

Robert Deignan
Founding partner of iS3
www.is3.com

Spyware and the Enterprise: The Problems, Costs, and Solutions

Writers of spyware create their programs for the money. Hackers, once satisfied with villainy as their reward, wrote viruses that brought them no financial gain. Now, they are going after the money, and it is enormously profitable. Profitability also means that writing malicious code has become attractive to well-financed organized crime and perpetrators of industrial espionage. If malicious attacks are not already being used as weaponry, they will be so used eventually. According to a report by Special Agent Wendi Whitmore, a computer crime and counterintelligence officer with the Air Force Office of Special Investigations, the military has seen a rise in such attacks over the last couple of years.

Because there is so much money to be made with it, spyware is here to stay. In the coming years, spyware techniques will change in nature and increase in technical sophistication — as will the technology to fight it.

Increasingly, enterprise applications are being downloaded. The browser has become the superhighway on which businesses' critical supplies are sent. When a browser is infected, the results are often disastrous.

On June 15, 2006, UPI Business News reported that more than 1,300 people in Oregon might become victims of identity theft because an employee of the Oregon Department of Revenue downloaded data-capturing spyware. The employee was using an office computer to surf pornographic sites and downloaded a Trojan horse. According to the report, this Trojan installed itself Jan. 5, 2006 and for the next four months stealthfully captured social security numbers, names, and addresses and relayed them back to its creator.

As a result of this security breach, The Oregon Department of Revenue has banned employees from accessing Web sites for personal use. This, however, is not a practical solution in many corporate environments where employees who use the vast resources of the Internet for appropriate purposes are equally vulnerable to spyware infection. For example, hackers can host bogus blog sites or create a blog on a legitimate host site and post Trojans or keylogging software to the page. It is only a matter of time before hackers find ways to take advantage of other flaws that could expose risk to all bloggers who subscribe to the pages' RSS feeds.

It is equally impractical to impose Internet access restriction on employees who work long hours and use their break times for online banking, shopping, and other personal business that might otherwise be neglected.

Why has no one yet found a way to eliminate spyware? Internet users are accustomed to hearing that spyware and other malware "exploit security holes" in operating systems. In fact, any application installed on a computer can perform any action the logged-in user is authorized to perform. To paraphrase Dr. Alan Karp, research team leader at Hewlett-Packard's Virus-Safe Computing Lab, there is no inherent reason why a solitaire game needs to be able to search the user's desktop, or why a spreadsheet program needs to be able to search its host's disk for secrets or put a Trojan in its startup folder. The levels of permission inherently granted to these applications are much higher than what is required to accomplish their tasks.

This is not to suggest that solitaire is using its authority for evil purposes, although it could. However, it logically follows that if there were an exploitable hole in solitaire, a spyware creator could gain control of this application and do anything that solitaire is authorized to do. Applications could have as much authority as they require and just enough time to accomplish their tasks; no more and no longer. The balancing act between functionality and security, known as "sandboxing," lies outside the scope of this book. It is noted only in that it helps to explain why spyware will not be eliminated any time soon and that network security must take this functionality into account.

Data Theft:
Problem

Increasingly, hackers are designing spyware specifically for identity theft. These programs compromise both personal and commercial privacy, with potentially dangerous effects for enterprises needing to protect proprietary information. When a computer is infected with spyware, all of the sensitive content, trade secrets, data, and passwords that reside on that computer are subject to theft. Spyware can be programmed to detect certain file types and then send the data in these files to an unauthorized third party. Keyloggers can read and broadcast everything typed on a keyboard, from a harmless e-mail to credit card account numbers and passwords to the administrative login passwords to a network.

Solution

Antispyware programs tailored toward businesses lock would-be thieves out of a system before they can access valuable data. Many of these stop all forms of spyware. When users first clean up their systems with certain programs, they remove existing spyware and prevent those threats from reinstalling themselves. With this protection, businesses can expand their use of computer technology to serve the company's business goals, instead of scaling back out of fear of data theft and fraud.

Loss of Employee Productivity:
Problem

The cost of spyware goes well beyond stolen data. It not only steals system resources, but also Internet bandwidth. It slows to a crawl the computer on which it is installed and can slow performance for other computers across a network. It can also cause a system to become unstable and crash. In the corporate environment, cleaning up employee machines loaded with spyware often accounts for 20 percent or more of an enterprise's IT help desk efforts.

Solution

Employees are rarely security experts, nor should they be. Without any time-consuming user intervention, antispyware continuously monitors desktops for spyware activity. With programs that operate in real time traditional scans are not needed and users are not interrupted by a lengthy, ultimately useless scanning process that allows spyware to re-install itself when users reboot.

Problem

Adware, although technically not spyware, is most effective when it is driven by spyware. If a user was surfing mortgage sites, an ad for a lender would bring better results than an ad for sports equipment. It is spyware that causes adware to deliver ads targeted to a user's surfing. Adware bombards employees with blizzards of pop-ups, often forcing browsers to close down. Worse, unsophisticated users might click on appealing ads, games, toolbars, or offers, thus downloading even more spyware. Many pop-up ads are keyed to certain products or services. By covering an entire screen, they can prevent users from navigating to intended sites.

Solution

Pop-ups can be vehicles for one of the most virulent spyware distribution schemes: the ActiveX drive-by download. Some antivirus programs include advanced pop-up protection that stops both adware and browser pop-ups. These programs enable workers to use their computers more efficiently, without the risk of inadvertent spyware installation.

Increased Bandwidth Costs:
Problem

Data flow to and from spyware has a cumulative effect on network performance. Spyware infesting a network uses valuable bandwidth when transmitting data back to its maker. Spyware transmits data about users' surfing habits to unauthorized third parties. Users' habits and preferences are analyzed and new content is sent back to the ad bank. The more spyware infects a system, the more the system pays. Botnets, which are spammers' latest "solution" to junk mail deterrence technologies, can turn users' machines into zombies, using all available bandwidth and slowing down entire networks.

Solution

By targeting spyware and preventing future installations, antispyware programs help conserve bandwidth. New ads are no longer downloaded to ad banks on machines and spyware reporting is halted. Without malicious spyware traffic, a company's bandwidth can be used for the purposes intended.

Poor System Performance:
Problem

Spyware is code, most of which is poorly written, causing the program to consume large amounts of memory. This can degrade computer performance drastically or even cause crashes. Unfortunately, many users believe this compromised performance is a result of an inadequate system and thus believe they need to invest in upgrading their systems.

Solution

Spyware makers do not care if their products have a harmful effect on their victims' computers. Their goals are to steal data or advertise their clients' products and services, which are at cross purposes with victims' goals. Antispyware programs detect, block, and quarantine spyware. They eliminate the possibility that unwanted spyware programs will ruin employees' machines or impair their performance.

The Tangible Cost of Spyware

How can one assess the loss of compromised data, stolen intellectual property, trade secrets, and customer data? According to iS3 researchers, various spyware attacks increased almost fourfold in 2005 and instances of Trojans more than doubled between 2005 and 2006. By the most conservative estimates and based on a limited survey, the FBI has determined that about 20 percent of U.S firms have experienced a cyber attack. The average cost per incident was $24,000 per company. These estimates are acknowledged to be low because most enterprises are reluctant to report successful breaches of their security. "Most companies that experience computer intrusions or breaches of security do not report the incidents to law enforcement," FBI Director Robert Mueller said at a Feb. 15 Business Software Alliance town-hall meeting.

Industry might be reticent to report spyware due to the belief that law enforcement cannot do very much to stop it and that the bad publicity would affect customer confidence and hence, profitability. In the short term, spyware does affect the bottom line. Long term, spyware undermines the public's faith in online commerce of all kinds.

Making the Investment

In a report published by Deloitte Touche Tohmatsu, more than half of all companies doing business in the technology, media, and telecommunications sectors have sustained data breaches that potentially exposed their intellectual property or customer information. Roughly one-third of those incidents directly resulted in financial losses.

Regulations such as the Sarbanes-Oxley Act, which mandates internal controls over financial reporting; HIPAA, which mandates protection for the privacy of personal health information; and the Graham-Leach-Bliley Act, which regulates sharing of personal information about individuals who obtain financial products or services from financial institutions, are showing benefits in improved business practices, but many IT professionals are concerned that with a focus on compliance, there are fewer dollars being allocated to robust network security.

Companies' reluctance to increase their spending on new security measures is serving them poorly. With the increasing proliferation and sophistication of spyware and other online threats, computer security needs to become an enterprisewide business concern, rather than a nuisance problem for IT.

*Robert Deignan is a founding partner of iS3 (**www.is3.com**) with a successful track record in marketing and sales. As executive vice president, Deignan is responsible for working with the iS3 executive team on the company's overall business strategy. He and his team are constantly analyzing sales and result data to identify trends, develop recommendations, and arm the sales, marketing, and development teams with business intelligence to guide future action steps. Deignan is responsible for working within all phases of the business to pinpoint new opportunities and to maximize the company's profits.*

CHAPTER 6

Web Browsers, Pop-Up Windows, & How to Surf the Web Safely

There are a variety of modern Web browsers to choose from and each offers advanced security and protection on the Web. Microsoft Internet Explorer has been a favorite target of malicious attacks and exploits in the past, but its latest version, Internet Explorer 8, boasts robust and significantly improved security over its predecessors. Internet Explorer and other major browsers will be explored later in this chapter.

Browsing the Web is dangerous. As you have discovered malware, viruses, worms, Trojan horses, and more are lurking, waiting to attack and infest computers and networks. As Web pages increased in interactivity and complexity, they spawned exploits and malware that have increased in frequency and volume as the Web grew in volume and use. Flash, Java, JavaScript, ActiveX, and other add-ons as well as database-driven Web sites dramatically improved functionality, appearance, and content presentation, but also opened up the door to even more malware exploits and hacking attempts. It is commonplace for users to have to download plug-ins to their browsers to enable advanced content or install third-party applications. Most of these are safe; however, the general rule of Web safety is to download only from trusted sources. This applies to downloads that are browser plugins or add-ons as well as normal software or file downloads. In the case of software or file downloads, most modern antivirus applications will scan these downloads before the download commences. When downloading files, users should save them to their hard drives first, then launch them, instead of clicking the "Open" button in the download dialog and having them launch on their own when the download is complete.

Passwords are a challenge to manage. Internet users have so many passwords today, to so many different Web sites that it is not easy to remember them all. Most modern browsers will help users do that by storing user names and passwords within the browser. This is safe to do, with some general rules. Users should employ good password techniques to create passwords that are not easy to crack, using special characters, letters, numbers, and a combination of upper and lower case characters.

Cookies, as mentioned previously, are small data files of information that are stored on a computer as users browse Web sites. Cookies usually contain some identifying information and other data that Web sites can use to "recognize" a user as a return site visitor. Cookies are not executable files; they are text-based files. Though they are not spyware or viruses, they are usually detected and removed by antispyware applications. Cookies are safe and they are necessary to display many Web sites, particularly those that are e-commerce-enabled to function properly.

Modern browsers give users the ability to accept or reject cookies. You can specify how your browser will handle cookies, and you can even accept or reject them as they are served during a user session on a Web site. If users choose to accept cookies, they can specify the length they are valid. It is best to use the default settings for cookies within a browser, which balance security with Web site interactivity and functionality. Five to ten years ago, cookies were a hot topic and many feared allowing cookies would allow hackers to break into computers or networks; however, this is not the case. Cookies cannot contain viruses, send e-mails, steal passwords, read files on a hard drive, or execute malware.

JavaScript is a scripting language that adds functionality to Web browsers. JavaScript is client-based, meaning the code must be inserted into the Web page that a user is visiting, and as the HTML/XHTML code is interpreted by the Web browser, it is read and executed within the browser. Each Web page contains HTML or XHTML code or formatting, which is read, executed, and interpreted by the Web browser and displayed back to you in the browser window in the proper display format. JavaScript can enable jump menus, validate form input, and rotate images based on mouse movements. Here is an example of a small piece of JavaScript:

```
<script language="javascript" type="text/javascript">
//<![CDATA[
var cot_loc0=(window.location.protocol == "https:")?
    "https://secure.comodo.net/trustlogo/javascript/cot.
    js" :
"http://www.trustlogo.com/trustlogo/javascript/cot.js";
document.writeln('<scr' + 'ipt language="JavaScript"
```

```
        src="'+cot_loc0+'" type="text\/javascript">'
        + '<\/scr'+ 'ipt>');
  //]]>
  </script>
```

This JavaScript code simply loads the "trusted logo" image for the secure certificate for the Web site into the browser window. In the following image, you can see the COMODO Authentic and Secure logo, which is loaded into the bottom right hand corner of the Web page and "floats" in this corner as the page is scrolled up and down. JavaScript enabled this and many more dynamic features on otherwise static Web pages.

JavaScript can be manipulated and can in fact try to launch malware if users find themselves on unscrupulous Web sites. Most browsers have the option to disable JavaScript.

Pop-up windows were very popular ten years ago, when every Web site had an annoying pop-up and browsers had no ability to block them. This is not the case today. Most Web sites do not use pop-ups, although many still use them for advertisement purposes. If users find many pop-ups in their browsing experiences, they likely have adware installed on their computers. Luckily, all modern Web browsers have built in pop-up blockers to combat these pesky windows. A virus or other malware infecting a computer can also cause pop-up windows. If users see pop-up windows, new toolbars in their Web browsers, changes to their browser's home page, or are being automatically redirected to other Web pages, they likely have malware running on their computers. Pop-ups, like other hyperlinks and banner advertising might be concealing malicious code or malware. Pop-ups are blocked by default in all modern Web browsers.

Malicious hackers can infect computers by exploiting incorrect or low security settings in a Web browser. Users should protect themselves by ensuring their Web browsers' security settings are properly set to "High" security.

It is important to note that high security settings might affect and limit functionality on some Web sites. If users have Web sites that do not function properly due to high security settings they can add them to the "trusted sites" list, which should restore full functionality. When a user adds a site to the trusted sites list in Internet Explorer, he or she should then set the security level to medium for the site to ensure full functionality. Users can run a test of their browsers' security at http://bcheck.scanit.be/bcheck, a free Web site that runs a full scan and provides users with a detailed summary report. Sample results from Mozilla Firefox and Internet Explorer follow

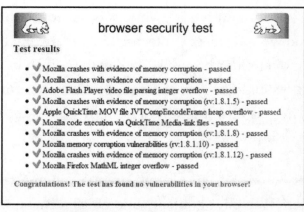

"Used with permission from Scanit"

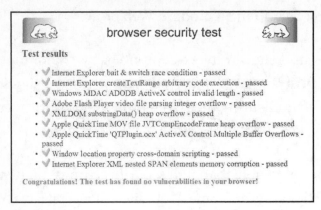

"Used with permission from Scanit"

Web Browsers

There are a variety of Web browsers on the market today and all are free. A Web browser is a software application for retrieving, presenting, and traversing information resources on the World Wide Web. Examples of these include Internet Explorer, Google Chrome, Opera, Apple Safari, and Mozilla Firefox. Despite the negative press Microsoft has received for its Internet Explorer, the latest rendition — Version 8 — is among the best. All of these browsers are modern, fast, and packed with features such as superior security and a wide variety of customization options. Most of today's browsers protect against malware, a major improvement over older browsers. No matter which browser users choose, they should be sure it is the latest version, with the latest patches. There is absolutely no reason to run older versions of modern Web browsers.

Today's browsers all have some unique differences; however, each renders Web pages quickly and efficiently. Google Chrome is a "light-weight" version browser, but runs quickly and efficiently. Chrome and Opera provide preview tabs. Mozilla Firefox is the most customizable browser with a wide variety of extensions and add-ons. Here is a brief look at the features for each major browser:

Firefox 3.6

Mozilla Firefox is a feature-rich, high performance, sleek-looking, and fast-loading browser. With a strong and loyal following, the number of extensions and customizations for Firefox is immense. Extensions and add-ons allow users to customize Firefox and add additional functionality. Of all the browsers available today, Firefox is by far the most customizable. The browser is very simple to use. Firefox 3.6 features a tabbed browser, integrated search, and enhanced security compared to previous versions. Users can check their Mozilla plug-ins — a small software program that extends the capabilities of a larger program — to make sure they have the latest versions here: www.mozilla.com/en-US/plugincheck/. You can download Firefox at www.mozilla.com.

Google Chrome 2.0

Google Chrome is sleek, fast, and lightweight, meaning it uses few system resources. Google Chrome is simple to use. It loads pages efficiently and displays them properly. Features include simplicity, the ability to search and navigate pages from the same window, and the ability to arrange tabs. Chrome is fast to launch, fast to load Web pages, and offers thumbnail views of users' favorite pages, which they can click on to launch. The thumbnail views are one of the best features of Chrome. Users also can download themes to customize the appearance of Chrome. Internet surfers can download Chrome at www.google.com/chrome.

Opera 10

Opera is sometimes found as a browser on smart phones. The full version for computers is packed with features, such as turbo speed for slow connections, tabbed views, and integrated Web search. It also features thumbnail previews and customized skins. Opera has built-in voice recognition, so it can follow voice commands for browsing and even read Web page content back to users. It has integrated search and customizable toolbars. Similar to Chrome, users can tile Web pages with thumbnail previews. Mouse gestures let users do frequently performed browser operations with small, quick mouse movements. The latest version of Opera seems to have remedied all of the previous version's shortfalls. Users can download Opera at www.opera.com.

Safari 5

Safari used to be Apple-exclusive; however, Safari 5 now runs on Microsoft Windows. Users who love Macs will probably want the Safari browser, which has the overall Mac look and feel. Like the others, it features tabbed browsing and is a "light" browser, which loads quickly and efficiently. Safari features a spell checker and resizable text boxes, a feature unique to the browser. "Top sites" is a nice feature that lets users see a preview of Web sites. Apple recently added antiphishing and antimalware to the Safari Web browser. Safari's strengths are its Mac-like appearance, speed, and minimal footprint. Internet surfers can download Safari at www.apple.com/safari.

Internet Explorer 8

Internet Explorer 8 boasts extensive security features, malware protection, phishing protection, and parental controls built in.

Internet Explorer 8 includes a wide variety of add-ons and customization options. Like other modern browsers, tabbed browsing is standard, as is integrated search. Internet Explorer 8 features a private browsing mode that prevents Web sites from tracking a site visit, recording name/passwords, and adding cookies or temporary Internet files. Internet Explorer 8 has built in accelerators to help users quickly perform everyday browsing tasks without navigating to other Web sites. Internet Explorer 8 comes with Windows 7, but can be downloaded for Windows XP and Windows Vista at www.microsoft.com/windows/Internet-explorer/ default.aspx.

So which browser is the best? Honestly, it comes down to personal preference and the features users want most. NSS Labs , a company that provides independent, unbiased analysis for internet security, completed tests using all major, modern Web browsers including Internet Explorer 8 for socially engineered malware. They state "Microsoft Internet Explorer 8 was the standout in our tests, achieving a best-in-class 69 percent catch rate against malware. It is clear that Microsoft is making an effort to provide security to their customers with IE8." The full report can be downloaded from http://nsslabs.com.

Internet users are at risk if they use older Web browsers and do not keep up with patches and upgrades. Most modern browsers will prompt users when new versions are released. Microsoft updates Internet Explorer through Microsoft Update, which is normally automated through the Windows control panel. You should make sure that Microsoft Update is always turned on. To do this, go to your Windows Control Panel and look for Windows Update in the System and Security Section. Users should make sure their browser's security settings are set at the highest level for most Web sites (and medium level for trusted sites in Internet Explorer) and they will be well-protected. PC Magazine completed a comprehensive review of Internet Explorer 8, determining that it offers more malware-detection features than other browsers. You can find the article in its entirety at www.pcmag.com/article2/0,2817,2328878,00.asp.

Windows 7 Parental Controls

A critical component to protecting a family's activity online might be the use of parental control software to monitor and restrict activity, particularly that of children. Parental controls let adult users restrict and limit what others can do on a computer and home network. They can prevent children from accessing offensive sites and restrict not only the total time they can access the Internet, but also control the times of day access is allowed. Parental controls are nothing new; they have been around for years. This software can be both standalone and integrated within a security suite. Earlier versions of the programs worked, but were not perfected, often blocking legitimate sites and, even worse, allowing access to offensive sites. Most if not all Internet security suites listed in Chapter 11 contain robust parental control software that is highly effective and easily customized to meet families' needs for a variety of operating systems.

Previous versions of Microsoft Windows have limited parental controls; however, this is an area in which Microsoft invested significant improvement and added functionality. Windows 7 offers parental control software that can be used at no additional charge, built into the operating system. Configuring parental controls in Windows 7 is simple, with access available through the control panel. First, users can select which programs younger users can access and which they cannot. Parents can control what "type" of games children can and cannot play, based on the Entertainment Software Rating Board's (ESRB) ratings of games. Similar to how movies are rated (G, PG, PG-13, R, and so on), games are ranked as well (Early Childhood, Everyone, Everyone (10+), Teen (13+), Mature (17+)). Parents can control what time of day children can use the computer and also what times of day the children can access the Internet. This controls total computer use, as well as Internet activity, within the day.

Web filtering is one of the most common features within any parental control. Filtering looks at the content of Web pages and filters them based on your specified parental control settings, blocking access to Web pages or specific content that is deemed inappropriate. In Windows 7, users can turn filtering on or off. If it is on, parents can choose settings from strict to basic or customize their control levels. Windows Live Essentials, which is a free add-on to Windows 7, lets users have even more control over Web site restrictions. Parents can also set up activity monitoring and automated reporting to scrutinize online activity. Additionally, they can control e-mail and instant messenger activity. You can download this at: http://download.live.com.

To help keep children safer online, parents should download Windows Live Family Safety. This free program helps users manage which Web sites children see and whom they can talk to online. It also provides helpful, easy-to-read reports of their online activity.

CHAPTER 7

Firewalls:
A Comprehensive Introduction

Computer users must have a reputable firewall installed on every computer that connects to the Internet or is part of a network. A firewall is software or hardware that is installed on computers or networks to block unauthorized access while still allowing authorized communications. A firewall acts as an intermediary between your computer and the Internet and is your first line of defense to prevent unauthorized access to your computer or network. Windows XP (Service Pack 2), Windows Vista, and Windows 7 come with firewalls built in, but there are many other options available to help protect users' computers and networks from malicious attacks and hackers. A firewall is a computer's primary defense against intruders. A firewall can come in a variety of options: software-based, hardware-based, built into Windows, third-party application, built into routers, and so on. This chapter is designed to give readers an in-depth introduction to firewalls, what they do, and why a user absolutely needs one.

It is the era of the Internet, and virtually any information is available at people's fingertips. There were more than 6.7 billion people in the world in 2009 and of those, more than 1.7 billion were active Internet users, an increase of more than 300 percent from 2000. The Internet's immense growth has fueled the information economy and as a result the world of e-commerce has exploded. Many businesses today have no brick and mortar storefront and rely entirely on an Internet presence. With a few clicks of a mouse, a person can purchase products without ever leaving home. The explosion of social networking sites has added to the Internet population boom.

The Internet is not a single network; rather, it is a vast collection of different networks spanning the globe. Internet protocols, particularly Internet protocol suite (TCP/IP), which is the protocol used for communications on the Internet, provide common services to users and facilitate communication between them. Whenever a person connects to the Internet via a personal computer, that computer becomes a part of this gigantic network. Whenever users connect to the Internet, they also expose their computers and networks to significant risk, if unprotected.

Cyber crime is rampant on the Internet. The Internet Crime Complaint Center (IC3) is an organization providing victims of cyber crimes an avenue to report criminal complaints. In 2009, there were 336,655 total complaints filed with IC3. This is a 22.3 percent increase compared to 2008, when 275,284 complaints were received. Nondelivery of merchandise was the most common complaint category, followed by identity theft, credit card fraud, auction fraud, and other types of fraud.

Basics of Information Security

Data is classified by three important characteristics:

- **Confidentiality:** Data must be incomprehensible to all users except the ones who are properly authorized to use it. In simple terms, only authorized users must be able to access data and it must be protected from unauthorized access or viewing.

- **Integrity:** Data integrity means data is reliable and authentic. Data integrity ensures data is trusted and complete.

- **Availability:** Availability ensures network data is available to all authorized users at any given time.

The loss of any of these three attributes can threaten the security of a network.

Internet Threats

Threats are becoming more innovative and skillful, which makes it harder for users to predict and intercept them, as well as ensure their computers have adequate security measures in place. Internet threats can be classified as:

Structured

Structured threats or attacks are well-planned. The assailants are skilled and well-aware of new technology and the latest exploits. They tend to attack by exploiting vulnerabilities in a system with available tools. If the tools are not available, they can create new ones to suit them. A structured attack can be carried out by non-computer ways, such as social engineering. Traditional defense methods often cannot help in avoiding and countering such threats to an Internet network.

Unstructured

Unstructured threats are less crucial than structured attacks; however, they still must be taken seriously. Unstructured threats are from unskilled and nonprofessional individuals, usually with little or no programming experience. Such people use tools that have been built by others to exploit vulnerabilities of a system.

The simplest way to protect against online security threats is to disconnect a computer from the Internet. Obviously, this is not a realistic solution. However, there are many ways a user can protect a computer from suspected threats. Most security measures employ data encryption and set passwords. Data encryption is a process that converts simple plain-text messages to encrypted cipher text. Cipher text is the encrypted form of plain text that is incomprehensible to anyone who is not authorized to view it. Therefore encrypted data cannot be read if intercepted, unlike unencrypted data, which can be intercepted, accessed, and read. A password, as most computer users know, is a secret word or phrase that gives a user access to a particular program or system. Another protection solution lies in installing a firewall.

What is a Firewall?

A firewall allows a person to use the Internet in his or her home, small business, or local area network while protecting against hackers, crackers, and other unauthorized users, preventing them from gaining access to the network and causing damage. A local area network (LAN) is a computer network in a physical area such as an office, home, or other small environment. A wide area network (WAN) covers a much larger area, such as large metropolitan areas. As stated earlier, a firewall is software or hardware that is installed on computers or networks to block unauthorized access while allowing authorized communications. A firewall acts as an intermediary between your computer and the Internet and is your first line of defense to prevent unauthorized access to your computer or network. A firewall can also be software-based, as is the case of the firewall built into Windows 7.

A firewall is a gatekeeper between a computer network or single computer and the Internet. It blocks certain traffic, incoming and outgoing, and monitors all activity to prevent unauthorized access. Most routers have built-in firewalls and, as discussed, Windows XP, Windows Vista, and Windows 7 have built-in software firewalls. A router is a hardware device that lets multiple wired or wireless networks connect. Most modern broadband routers filter incoming and outgoing traffic and act as a network switch and a hardware firewall. Most wireless routers will connect to incoming broadband connections, such as cable modems and can be set up to broadcast wireless Internet access signals for wireless devices to join the network. Routers also allow network-enabled devices, such as network printers, to connect to the network and be accessible from any computer on the network.

Broadband routers act as Dynamic Host Configuration Protocol (DHCP) servers. DHCP is a protocol that assigns unique IP addresses to devices connected to the network automatically and then releases and renews these addresses as your devices leave or re-join the network, such as wireless laptops, which join the network when in use and leave the network when disconnected. Because a broadband router provides wireless capability, DHCP servers act as a network switch and also provide you with a built-in firewall. They are a great investment for any home or small business network and can be bought for less than $100.

On larger, more advanced networks, a firewall might be installed on a standalone computer and actively monitored. In most homes and small businesses, the firewall includes both hardware (a router) and software (an operating system or third-party program). Firewalls range from very simple to very sophisticated, depending upon a user's requirements and system configuration. Firewalls are usually employed at organization levels to protect intranets. Businesses use firewalls to protect against any unwanted user intrusion and to limit employees' access to the Internet or extranet.

Most software firewalls also include parental controls to manage what kinds, when, and for how long children visit Web sites. Some Internet security packages will also allow users to block inappropriate content and pictures and specific text content they do not want children to view.

How do Firewalls Work?

A firewall filters the traffic to and from a computer or private network to the Internet. In a circuit-switched network like telephone systems, the network between the two end users is established and reserved. Such a reserved path or circuit is used for the communication of the users only; no one can send or receive data on it. As discussed previously, the Internet is a packet-switched network, meaning that the data is broken up into "packets" and then transmitted across the Internet in small pieces. To transfer data across a network, these packets of information are transmitted separately and independent of one another. Breaking the information into smaller pieces allows many systems to share the network. All data transfer across IP networks happens in the form of packets. Firewall technology employs the following methods for controlling the in and out flow of data to and from the network:

Packet filtering

Packet filtering selectively routes packets between the internal and external hosts. The site employing the packet filtering specifies the conditions it uses to filter information. By analyzing the incoming and outgoing packets and comparing them to the IP addresses of the source and destination hosts, you can prevent packets from being intercepted, altered, or modified and exchanged for the original packet. Packet filtering is one way firewalls help to ensure incoming and outgoing data transmission are secure and have not been tampered while transmitting across the Internet.

Proxy server

Proxy servers are also called application-level gateways — an intermediary between your computer and your destination Web server on the Internet. A firewall host can run proxy services to provide security. Proxy services act as an intermediate communicator that take in requests for the Internet service from the user and forward them to actual service providers, providing a layer of security between you and your destination. The destination Web site will never see your computer on the site or accessing the server. Instead, it will see the proxy server. Therefore, the proxy server provides replacement services and acts as a gateway between a network and the Internet. Proxy services are capable of caching — or storing data for faster retrieval — and increasing performance. Proxy services can be called intelligent filters.

Stateful inspection

In this technique, instead of the firewall only looking at the data contents and the packets, stateful inspection tracks each connection of the firewall and examines not only the packet and the IP addresses of the sender and recipient, but also the header and the actual contents of the packet for validity. In stateful inspection, key fields are matched with the criteria selected when configuring and setting up the firewall. Information traveling from inside the firewall to the outside is monitored and the incoming packet is compared to legitimate packets. If the comparison yields a reasonable match the data is allowed through; if not, it is discarded. The firewall is programmed to test for the validity of the packets from different connections. IP-spoofing and port-scanning attacks can be minimized using stateful inspection.

Virtual Private Networks

A virtual private network (VPN) is a network that passes internal information packets to a public network so the packets of data are protected using encryption. VPN connections let computers establish secure communication from the Internet into an internal company network or intranet. Firewalls can be used in conjunction with routers to establish safe VPNs for home and small business use as well, letting users remotely access data in a secure environment.

Types of Firewalls

A firewall can be a classified as a hardware or software firewall. A firewall acts as an intermediary between your computer and the

Internet and is your first line of defense to prevent unauthorized access to your computer or network.

Software firewall

Any ordinary computer running any common operating system can use firewall software. Software firewalls can be integrated into the operating system or third-party solutions. In general, software firewalls are very effective and easy to configure. Internet surfers can use a software firewall in addition to a hardware firewall.

Hardware firewall

A hardware firewall is typically a device that users connect between a network's computers and a broadband modem or other Internet connection. Hardware firewalls can be expensive, dedicated firewall devices or can be built into more affordable devices, such as routers.

Open source & commercial firewalls

Open source is a software license model wherein the source code is available to anyone at no cost. Often, the terms of use allow for altering, modifying, and redistributing the code. Commercial software is software developed and licensed for use for a fee. Users have to pay a registration fee to "activate" the license. Users can typically use a 30-day trial version or limited-functionality version. To get full functionality, users must pay the registration fee. The commercial entity often provides support, training, updates, and other similar services needed by customers to effectively use the software. The source code is typically not made available to the user. Free options might be pretty good, but they are not recommended firewalls because computer and network security is worth investing in. Open source or freeware firewalls often leave users open to attack and, unlike commercial software that benefits from routine updates, open source might or might not be updated and patched.

Firewalls: Home and Business Networks

It is a misconception that home computer users are less prone to online risks and threats. Home users share the same kinds of risks business users face, although they are often less attractive targets. When selecting firewall software, users must analyze the threat. Home computer users should establish a security policy at home, just as they do for a small business. The security policy at a home must take into account the type of activities users perform. Users should disable unneeded communication ports to prevent their exploitation.

A security policy must assure no spontaneous incoming traffic, such as a denial of service attack, is allowed onto a network. A business security policy must ensure all employees utilize personal firewall software and updated antivirus and antimalware. Users should require the same of contractors and others who might use their networks. Employees should not store sensitive work-related data on the computers in their homes. When working with a personal firewall, users' immediate concern is ease of use and ease in configuring the firewall. It is critical to establish timely alert notification and automated updates.

An Introduction to Hardware and Software Firewall Products

Taking into account the threats to Internet security today, many leading vendors have come up with flexible and secure firewalls. There are many choices, and it is important for users to do some research in advance to ensure that a firewall is the best for their organization and specific security policies. Not all firewalls are created the same.

Firewalls are typically classified as personal, for homes or small businesses, or professional, typically used by larger corporations, banks, and government. Hardware firewalls are relatively expensive and used in commercial applications to fight major threats to larger and more complex networks. Some of the more popular hardware based firewalls vendors are WebRamp, Sonic Wall, Cisco, and D-Link.

Cisco

Cisco is a major contender in networking and Internet security. It has many programs that serve different sized networks from home office organizations to companies with more than 50,000 computers.

WebRamp 1700

Some of the best solutions for the small office or home network are provided by Rampworks. WebRamp offers industry-leading firewall protection against network security violations and security to users that want to be perpetually connected to the Internet. WebRamp is designed for small offices and can be used in homes. WebRamp features stateful packet inspection, protecting you from denial of service and other forms of attacks.

SonicWall Pro

Small- to medium-sized networks can be made more secure by using Sonic firewall technologies. SonicWall's firewall is usually installed by universities to prevent students from getting access to unwanted sites and offices where staff is limited in where they can surf the Internet. It is also used to protect sensitive military organizations. The best feature of SonicWall's firewall is that it is easy to install and configure without requiring much technical knowledge.

FireBox

FireBox is another hardware-based firewall by Watch Guard. It aims to provide cost-effective and comprehensive messaging security. This firewall is for midsize businesses. The firewall facilitates faster hardware VPN encryption for larger networks.

OfficeConnect

OfficeConnect Firewall by 3Com is a hardware firewall built for small networks for up to 25 users. The firewall aims to protect users by blocking unauthorized network access and preventing DoS attacks. The firewall enables the administrator to control and monitor Internet access by users connected to the network. OfficeConnect is an efficient Internet security system that is affordable, simple to install, and easy to use.

Next is a quick look at some personal firewall software applications.

Microsoft Windows firewalls

Windows provides a firewall that is included in the operating system. It was made a part of the OS in Windows XP Service Pack 2 and Windows 2003 server. The firewall is intended to provide the following features to users:

- Alert the user about incoming connection attempts.

- Stop unsolicited network traffic and hide a computer from it. Users should not respond to unwanted network requests and traffic.

- Monitor applications that are listening for incoming connections and take care of all incoming Internet users.

- Prompt the user if any locally installed application makes an attempt to connect to the Internet and also provide the information about the destination where the application wishes to communicate.

Systems running Windows XP, Windows Vista, or Windows 7 have a built in firewall turned on by default.

Windows XP firewall

Users with Windows XP Service Pack 2 have three options in the Windows Security Center. They are:

- Firewall
- Automatic Updates
- Antivirus

Users should enable the built-in firewall prior to setting up an Internet connection. It is relatively simple to detect any Internet connection. The basic functions the Windows XP firewall will do are:

- Allow users to share files or a printer between two computers in a local area network setup.

- Block any attempts from people on the Internet to access a computer.

The firewall in Windows XP is very simple and, although better than nothing, is not a good solution for multiple-user computer networks and it should be replaced with a third-party firewall solution.

Windows Vista firewall

The firewall in Windows Vista has more advanced features than that in Windows XP, such as Windows Defender and malware protection. Windows Defender is a utility that blocks pop-ups and protects against security threats. Though it is not nearly as robust as commercially available firewalls, it provides basic, out-of-the-box firewall protection.

It is important to regularly monitor a firewall and ensure it is enabled and working. To do this, Windows Vista users should simply go to the Control Panel, then "Security," and access the firewall settings. This Windows firewall has two different interfaces. The default firewall interface is the same as in the Windows XP firewall. In Vista, the firewall is turned on by default. The basic interface shows settings and configuration details.

To view and configure advanced settings, users need to create a custom Microsoft Management Console (MMC) to control access to the firewall's advanced settings. To create an MMC, one should open the Start Menu and the RUN application, type "mmc.exe," and then hit "Enter." Select "File" and "Add/Remove Snap-in." Open the Available Snap-ins list and locate the entry "Windows Firewall With Advanced Security." Select the option and then click the "Add" button. Select the default settings and hit "OK." Once users have created the MMC, they can use the Advanced tab, which provides significantly more control over the firewall. After setting up the MMC users can make custom profiles. Users can set up different profiles and customize them according to the situation. They can create rules blocking or allowing certain programs or ports. Users can also modify the already existing pre-configured rules. Again, the firewall in Windows Vista is good for the basic home user, but it would be better to replace it with a third-party commercial firewall.

Windows 7 firewall

The firewall in Windows 7 is much more advanced than the previous Windows versions and actually quite effective. Although it is not the most powerful or customizable firewall software available, it provides robust features and tight integration into the Windows operating system. The interface is simple compared to other firewalls and the features are very easy to understand and manage, unlike some other firewalls. The Windows 7 firewall will now allow users to access advanced settings, which includes configuration of filtering for outgoing connections through the Control Panel. Of course, because it is part of the operating system, the firewall is completely free and supported by Microsoft for future updates or patches.

Although the Windows 7 firewall is adequate for most home and small business users, many will opt for a third-party firewall solution. *Some commercial firewall recommendations are available in this chapter and in Chapter 11.*

Use caution when allowing exceptions to firewall rules. An exception, in the case of a firewall, occurs when you specifically allow a certain action to take place, despite the existence of a rule, such as the opening of a certain port or allowing a specific IP address to access your network. An exception will allow the data traffic to flow unfiltered through the firewall, which might be required for some applications, such as instant messengers. Users should allow exceptions only when truly needed and once no longer required, remove the exception. Too many exceptions expose a system to attack. Users should never allow an exception for a program they do not recognize. Users can customize the firewall based on filtering by protocol, domain name, or IP address. This helps filter out unauthorized traffic or intrusion attempts quickly.

The Microsoft Windows firewall, which is turned on by default in Windows XP (SP2) and higher, is by far the most widely used firewall. One important weakness in the Windows Firewall is that it only monitors incoming traffic, not outgoing. If your users have malware sending traffic out on their computers, Windows Firewall will not detect it, block it, or notify users.

Norton Internet Security Suite 2010

This suite includes a personal firewall and protection from phishing, worms, viruses, intrusions, and other spyware. Other enhancements include pop-up blockers, parental controls, and the blocking of personal information. *PC World* magazine (**www. pcworld.com**) ranked it as the No. 1 overall Internet security suite in the December 2009 issue. Norton 360™ Version 3.0 is an improved version that protects against viruses, worms, hackers, and botnets and safeguards against online identity theft, file protection, and performance tuning.

ZoneAlarm Pro

This popular firewall is now available in multiple languages. The ZoneAlarm OS Firewall monitors behaviors within a computer to spot and stop even the most sophisticated new attacks that bypass traditional antivirus and security suites. It defeats new, advanced attacks and restricts programs from malicious activities, blocking attacks that bypass other defenses. OS Firewall proactively protects against inbound and outbound attacks, making users invisible to hackers. Additionally, it detects wireless networks and automatically applies the most secure firewall protection setting. ZoneAlarm also provides users with identification-protection services and monitors users' credit reports daily with e-mail alerts and reports.

ESET Smart Security

Proactive detection that augments ESET Smart Security is a smart technology to protect users from Internet threats. It blocks most known and undiscovered threats. It is very robust compared to other technologies. Smart Security stops most new threats proactively. It has an integrated antispam and personal firewall, scans and cleans Internet traffic and e-mail, and prevents malware from infecting your system.

Kaspersky Internet Security

Kaspersky Internet Security 2009 includes components such as an antivirus scanner, antispyware scanner, and firewall. These features are incorporated into the control panel interface that is easy to use and very tidy. All the integrated features work quiet well and this is indeed great software to protect your computer and network.

Comodo Firewall + Antivirus for Windows

Comodo Firewall blocks suspicious files, stops viruses, and has automatic updates to keep computers fully protected. Comodo provides users with basic protection, for free.

Online Armor

Online Armor is another free firewall that offers basic protection but does not have automatic updates. The premium edition, Online Armor ++, includes powerful antivirus and antispyware capabilities. Online Armor's personal firewall stops hackers, stops malicious programs, protects users when banking and transacting online, and protects users' identities.

Sunbelt Personal Firewall

Sunbelt offers a robust firewall to protect users from hackers. Recent changes include improvement in network performance, improvement in packet filtering, enhanced process injection preventing code injection attempts, and updated intrusion-detection rules, which provide enhanced protection against SQL injection and solid defense against intrusion attempts from the Internet.

Norman Personal Firewall

Norman Personal Firewall is highly rated and works very effectively. Norman uses computer and port stealthing technology so that your computer is not visible to potential hackers. It offers robust hacker protection, stateful packet inspection, and two-way traffic control for both incoming and outgoing network traffic and is highly customizable.

OutpostPro Firewall

OutpostPro Firewall is an advanced software firewall with built-in antispyware that provides superior protection against hackers and other online threats. This two-way firewall monitors both inbound and outbound connections to prevent authorized network access. Like many other firewall products, it makes your computer invisible on the Internet and shields it from attack.

A firewall alone does not provide complete security; however, it is a computer's first and best initial line of defense against intruders and hackers. Although this chapter merely brushed the surface of firewalls, the key points are that users must have an active firewall running on their computers and it is recommended they also have a network router to protect them from attacks. Firewalls alone do not assure complete security. In addition to a firewall, substantial measures must be taken to ensure physical (protection of computers, servers, and network systems) and host server security. Moreover, it is important to educate network users about security to strengthen an overall security plan.

Firewalls cannot protect against completely new threats; as the methods of attacks become more complex, firewall technology evolves. For the novice, firewalls can be annoying by blocking legitimate traffic or applications, and a common mistake is to disable them to avoid these interruptions. This is a mistake and leaves a computer or network open to attack. Users should never connect a computer to the Internet that does not have an active firewall running. Lastly, keep in mind that a firewall cannot do it all; users still need powerful antivirus, antimalware, antispyware, and antispam software to protect each computer in your network.

CHAPTER 8

Hackers: How to Defend Against Hacks & Other Attacks

Hacking is a term that encompasses many different (and often times conflicting) definitions, all of which provide a rather skewered and negative perspective of the computing industry as a whole. Nowadays, the most common stereotype surrounding the term "hacking" and its noun, "hacker," is that of a delinquent or criminal subculture that seeks to circumvent the security systems that protect computer networks. This deceptively simple definition poses more questions than answers, because in some jurisdictions the mere act of bypassing the security of a computer is considered criminal. In other areas there is a requirement that damage had to be inflicted or a substantiated loss, financial or otherwise, sustained. Such legal ambiguity has confused the public's perception even further regarding who a hacker is, what hacking is, and the legal implication of being a hacker or attempting to hack into a computer or network.

Within the computing industry and community, the term hacking and hacker is used in a more benign, possibly even flattering, manner to describe a person who is technically adept and has both the will and ability to improve his or her computing skills and functions. Hackers seek to work with current technology and improve it by identifying and correcting inherent software design flaws and exposing computer and network security threats to an individual, business, or other organization. In this respect, many mainstream computing experts have been labeled as hackers or have engaged in hacking when the intent is not malicious. These individuals attempt to identify potential threats and offer solutions to correct them before someone else identifies them and exploits them for malicious gain. A "white hat" hacker is a good guy, who tries to identify and solve security problems, and a "black hat" hacker tries to exploit security flaws for financial gain or other malicious intent (such as infiltration, damage, or destruction).

Part of the confusion about hackers also stems from the fact the computing subculture is a rich and nuanced community. A similar term is "cracking," specifically refers to the process of crippling the antipiracy mechanisms of commercially available software and circumventing it in an attempt to allow unfettered access and usage of the software. Cracking or piracy of software is illegal.

There is a fine line between an enthusiastic computer networking expert and a hacker, and the computing community concedes that the defining characteristic between the two is simply a matter of intent. Black hat hacking is the infiltration, covert or otherwise, of a computer network or system with the specific intention of maliciously causing damage to it. White hat hacking, on the other hand, is a security audit of a computer system or network to more readily identify key weaknesses within it and therefore remedy them so the entire system is more robust as a whole. There are several companies who specialize in white hat hacking and whose purpose is to identify and help fix any potential security flaws in a computer or network's operations to prevent against black hat infiltration. This distinction has itself courted no shortage of controversy, especially among law enforcement and legal communities that feel such rationalization is little more than an attempt to legitimize a criminal offense.

Another facet of the hacker stereotype is the assumption that all hackers are technically gifted and skilled at what they do. There is an entire subgroup of hackers referred to as "script kiddies," which is a term of contempt typically used to refer to individuals who download and run scripts created and coded by others. Script kiddies use these materials to manipulate computer systems with little to no actual knowledge of what the codes and scripts actually do. This general knowledge is good to have so users can classify between black hat hackers, white hat hackers, crackers, and script kiddies.

Methods Hackers Use to Attack

The methods hackers utilize in an attempt to infiltrate and or sabotage a computer network are widely varied. Even a rudimentary appreciation for their most commonly relied upon methods will help ensure users are safeguarded against the most damaging effects and risks of a hacking attack. Some of the following methods are applicable in a general sense, but others will only be utilized in specific circumstances, depending on hardware and network configuration, operating systems, and so forth.

SQL injection

Search Query Language (SQL) is a powerful programming language typically used for data manipulation, such as searching, filtering, storing, and altering large volumes of data of any kind. Any sort of membership-driven Web site, such as a social networking or dating site in which the users submit their personal details, relies upon SQL or some other equivalent language. As the name would suggest, the SQL-injection hacking method literally "injects" malicious, harmful code into the SQL query, which the hacker uses for a particular, desired effect.

Maliciously minded users commonly create a "superuser" or administrator account with an the SQL injection. This account will grant them full permission and access rights with which they can manipulate the database far easier and extract critical, sensitive information. This means they can delete entire segments of the database, or even the database itself, at their leisure. SQL injection is only a security concern and risk if the Web site owner has implemented SQL in his or her Web site design and the Web site is running an SQL server for database interactivity. The attack is typically utilized against poorly coded Web sites that have been made by inexperienced Web designers. Thankfully, as easy as it to implement a SQL-injection attack, it is equally straightforward to prevent it as well.

The method of safeguarding against SQL injection attacks is used to ensure a properly coded Web site. You should have your Web site developer validate that your site has been tested for any SQL injection exploits and is properly protected.

Password cracking

Password cracking is something of a misleading moniker because it conjures up images of a computer system having its password circumvented or bypassed in some illicit manner. In reality, this is merely a facet of the password-cracking process. Password cracking also encompasses the unauthorized recovery or retrieval of passwords for sensitive areas, in addition to the methods actually employed to achieve such results. Password cracking is achieved in a number of different ways.

First is the rather curiously named "social engineering," which refers to the process whereby a malicious user will attempt to guess a particular password, either by exploiting what he or she already knows about the person responsible for creating the current password or the items people tend to rely on when choosing a password. People will either simply keep the default password associated with a particular computer system or software package (for example, "password"), or will choose a password that has some sort of relevance and degree of sentimentality associated with it, such as their birthday, the name of their spouse, a favorite pet, or favorite color.

For example, the Web server application package XAMPP features a default password of "root." XAMPP is a tool that was created to allow Web developers and designers to test their Web sites on their computers without requiring access to the Internet. By design, most security protections are removed to enable this functionality. A number of this program's users simply neglect to alter the default settings, exposing their computers to significant risk. The best way to circumvent social engineering tricks is to ensure a password is more than six characters long and includes a combination of not only alphabetical and numerical characters, but also special characters, such as "!," "@," "#," ";," "?," "|," "\," ")," "(,""&," and "*." This small precaution will exponentially increase a password's strength, because it makes social engineering effectively useless and also makes brute-force attacks much harder to implement.

This leads to the next form of attack commonly utilized and implemented in password cracking: "brute forcing," which is a strategy to break the encryption of secure data. Rather colorfully named, brute forcing also happens to be a fairly accurate summary of what this technique involves, because there is no degree of finesse or sophistication involved. The following example is the best way to describe brute forcing:

BRUTE FORCE EXAMPLE
A person is confronted with an ATM or other form of cash withdrawal machine and wishes to gain unauthorized access to an account that they do not have permission to access. Given that all personal identification numbers (PINs) are of a specified length, in theory, and by a steady process of trial and error, the malicious user will be able to gain access to the bank account if he or she tries every single pin combination that exists in the world. The person will eventually stumble upon the right number, because there are a limited number of options. When it comes to the password cracking method of brute forcing, the old adage of "if at first you don't succeed, then try, try again" suits the situation. There are a number of dedicated software application packages with colorful names such as "Brutus" and "John the Ripper" that specifically perform the number generation needed to find passwords.

A brute-force attack will typically occurs in one of three essential ways:

Manual submission

In this type of attack, a malicious user will manually enter the repeated attempts to log in without using a software package.

Dictionary-based attacks

Dictionary-based attacks use computer programs or scripts that combine words in a dictionary as well as numbers to try each and every variation.

Generated logins

Generated logins also rely on computer programs or scripts that generate usernames and number sequences then try these in succession. The distinction between these and dictionary-based attacks is slight; typically, generated logins are based on establishing user name protocols — standardized naming methodology for user names. For example, a protocol might include: First Initial, Middle Initial, Last Name plus the domain name, or bcbrown@brucecbrown.com. If John Smith worked at this company, his user name would be jsmith@brucecbrown.com. By identifying user name protocols, this potentially eliminates the guesswork involved in identifying the naming convention for every user name in the business or organization.

Brute forcing is, to the novice computer security expert, an extremely daunting and intimidating threat, because, theoretically, a brute-force attack can circumvent any security system given sufficient time. However, security personnel who are concerned about the integrity of their systems, should consider the following:

- Brute forcing is a laborious, time-consuming process that will be readily identifiable within the computer logs. Although two or three failed log in attempts can be chalked up to human error, several hundred thousand log-in attempts all within quick succession of one another can be safely attributed to something much less benign.

- One of the fundamental aspects of a brute-force attack is that it specifically requires the means to try every single password variation. By limiting the number of tries a user gets to enter a password, systems render a brute-force attack powerless. Like all great ideas and solutions, such a simple counter measure really is the key to stopping a brute-force attack dead in its tracks.

- A brute-force attack will typically require physical access to the computer system in question for the malicious user to input the passwords. Although you can access online passwords with remote access, physical access is essential for any offline attempts. Maintaining a degree of physical security, including closed-circuit televisions, locked and or alarmed doors, and roaming patrols, will also significantly reduce the odds of malicious individuals using such an attack.

- Most novice computer users argue that having a password is a waste of time, given that brute force can simply crack it given enough time. Although there can be no denying the truth of this statement, it is important to note that a brute-force attack is time-consuming. Amateur hackers and people concerned with being detected and apprehended usually do not use brute force attacks either.

- If the attack is via remote access and is being directed towards an Internet server, then the best way to stop the attack is simply to ban the IP address or IP range — an established set of sequential IP addresses — of the person who is attempting to log in. This particular countermeasure by itself provides only a limited amount of protection, because the malicious user/hacker can quickly circumvent such a security measure using an Internet proxy server or software package that will alter his or her IP address. However, if this security measure is used in conjunction with the limited login approach, this effectively stops the brute-force attacking from happening.

Port/vulnerability scanning

Port scanning, using computer software designed to probe a particular computer network for open "ports," is another form of hacking. Port scanning is used as a diagnostic tool both by legitimate computer security personnel as well as malicious users. Ports, in the context of computing, are a means of communication relayed between Internet protocols. Every computer process/program will be given a specific port or range of ports with which it can more readily communicate. Although some might regard this as little more than an exercise in semantic wordplay, it should be noted that the phrase "port scanning" refers specifically to the scanning of a single port that might be able to be exploited, while "port sweeping" refers to the scanning of multiple ports simultaneously.

Packet analyzers/sniffers

Packet sniffers are software or hardware designed to intercept, analyze, and log traffic flowing over a network, such as the Internet. Packet sniffers can be computer hardware peripherals, computer software packages, or a combination of the two. Their sole purpose is to intercept data packets as they are relayed across a network, to allow the operator of the packet analyzer to read the packets' contents. Packet sniffers are of special concern when it comes to wired-LAN networks because the entire traffic — a term for relaying data packets over a network — of the network can be compromised with access to only one terminal within the entire network. To safeguard the network's integrity, it is imperative the owner and administrator responsible for the network ensure there are no weak links that be easily accessed.

Packet sniffers are akin to a wire tap on a phone; although, unlike a wire tap, which simply records the information being relayed over the telephone connection, the packet sniffer actually converts the raw data being transmitted over the network into a legible form that humans can read. One of the most frustrating aspects about packet sniffers is that, although they excel in intercepting data packets, they do not actually transmit data themselves, which makes their detection all the more difficult without specialized counter-packet sniffing items. One of the most effective ways to draw out an enemy sniper is to draw his attention toward a false target. With his attention so diverted he will blow his cover, thereby allowing you to direct your fire toward him. In the same manner, when it comes to trying to detect and foil a potential packet sniffer, the network administrator might want to leave a "honey trap," which is a computer server intentionally left seemingly defenseless. This server will audit and record salient information about the hacker attacking the network, such as his or her IP address and the software used to intercept the network's traffic.

There are a number of specialized computer programs you can rely on to detect the presence of an inappropriate or harmful packet sniffer, including:

- AntiSniff (**www.packetstormsecurity.org/sniffers/anti-sniff**),
- Ifstatus (**http://ifstatus.sourceforge.net**)
- Neped (**www.securiteam.com/tools/2GUQ8QAQOU.html**).

Given the inherent difficulties associated with detecting and foiling packet sniffers, and also the potential costs associated with such measures, the most powerful weapon in the network administrator's arsenal is knowledge. By educating users about the various protocols to use (for example, which protocols are secure and which are not), network administrators can significantly reduce their workloads. Do not make packet sniffing any easier for a malicious user. Make sure that any and all unused and unneeded ports in a computer are shut down, and that port mirroring is also disabled if it is not currently being used. Ensure that a good firewall is installed at all times to cloak a computer's access ports. It is entirely possible for a current network device, such as a router or computer, to become manipulated by a malicious user for harmful purposes; therefore, it is imperative the devices are password-protected to prevent such manipulations.

Why do People Hack?

The reasons that compel people to hack computer networks are as varied as the methods they use, so it is difficult to narrow down a specific list of factors that compel people to hack. But, you can study the reasons people have cited. For some, hacking is a form of intellectual sabotage, an act of arrogance designed to show their "superior" skills and knowledge to their hapless victims. As such, hacking has been compared to a form of cyber voyeurism (hackers access secure servers and networks simply because they are not supposed to be there). This is a factor often attributed most specifically to the "script kiddy" generation.

For other hackers, their motivations have more sinister twist. They want unauthorized access to secure networks and servers to achieve one goal: to acquire sensitive, damaging, or critical information. This can be for criminal reasons, to further terrorist activities, or even as part of industrial espionage, whereby competitors seek to gain an unfair advantage over a rival by stealing trade secrets. Others will perpetrate such attacks simply to deface, vandalize, or otherwise cause alarm, annoyance, and distress to the victim for political, racial, and ideological motivations, or simply as an expression of revenge. Perpetrators might be disgruntled employees who are dissatisfied at being terminated from their jobs or students who have been expelled from an educational institution.

There are also computer security experts who conduct a battery of hacking tricks and methods in an attempt to more readily identify the weaknesses and security gaps within the current security regime either as part of their employment, for recreational reasons, or to secure their own personal computers or networks. This last category has been listed in distinction from the others to further shatter the notion that hacking is always a criminal or harmful activity. In reality, hacking is entirely contingent upon the hackers themselves and what their intentions are. Hackers can, and do, perform an essential function by identifying security gaps, whether such identification is deliberate or purely incidental.

Protections Against Hacking

Please note that there is no single solution to the issue of protecting against hackers and their nefarious deeds, and it is never possible to be 100 percent hacker-proof. That said, users can ensure they implement sufficient layers of protection that will deter and defend against most hackers, forcing them to find other targets. Never underestimate the power of deterrence when it comes to fending off the would-be hackers, because they achieve their mischief specifically by exploiting and relying upon a lack of knowledge and security on the part of individuals, businesses, and governments.

Though previous sections of this chapter highlighted specific counter measures for some of the different methods of hacking, there is more generalized advice users can implement, regardless of the their types of network. Users should ensure data access and administrative rights are limited solely to those people who actually need this high level of access. This should be implemented not only in relation to the computer terminals themselves, but also in relation to the physical access to network computers and servers. Even a simple precaution, such as a locked room and a single key to that room, can be effective means of preventing disgruntled employees from wreaking harm.

Users might want to consider hiring a computer or Web site security expert to test their sites or computers and determine what vulnerabilities exist. A little bit of knowledge can sometimes be more counterproductive than none at all; novices assume the rudimentary safety precautions they have implemented will be sufficient to keep hackers at bay. The advice of a professional might be a wise security investment for your company. Anyone can be a victim of hacking attacks, even "secure" federal agencies such as the National Security Administration and Central Intelligence Agency.

CHAPTER 9

Network Security: How to Protect and Secure your Home or Small-business Network

This chapter is designed to give an in-depth introduction to network security and how to protect home or small-business networks from malicious attacks. Although Chapter 10 is dedicated to wireless network security and firewalls, this chapter is critical to help users ensure they have a secure network for their homes or small businesses. Network security is a specialized area of networking that includes provisions for maintaining the security of the computer network infrastructure. It also includes the policies and procedures that users or network administrators establish to protect a computer network and the resources that are accessible to intruders through the network. Network security applies to both home and small-business networks, although it is usually associated with the latter.

Networks, in terms of information technology, are a group of computers that are connected to each other. Computers can be connected to each other through various media, such as phone lines, USB ports, wireless connections, or Ethernet connections

— established when you are connected to a wired or wireless network. This connection forms a small network, which in turn is connected to bigger and bigger networks. This potpourri of networks forms the Internet.

There are more and more people accessing the Internet each day and, in theory, there are innumerable computers potentially connected to a user. As they log on to the Internet, users need to be aware of the possible threats to their own networks. Protecting a network from any such possible intrusion threat from the Internet is called network security. Network security requires a constant and steady monitoring of security measures to maintain and protect the usability, integrity, and reliability of the network and the data on the network. Many times network security and information security are used interchangeably. However, network security is just the first step toward information security. Information security deals with any kind of threat toward data loss, be it an external intruder, malware, or a human error by an authorized user. Network security, on the other hand, deals with security of the boundaries of a home or office network. It prohibits any kind of malware or hacker and protects the network from any threat to its security.

Today, there are several threats all across the Internet that can harm a computer network. Some of the most common ones that affect nearly all organizations, be they big or small, are:

- Viruses, worms, Trojan horses
- Hackers
- Malware (spyware and adware)

- Zero day/zero hour attacks — an attack against a computer vulnerability for which no known fix has been released
- Data theft and data interception
- Identity theft

All of these threats can cause serious harm to a computer or network, such as deleting or changing a file or its parts, sending crucial information from a victim's system to an outsider, and not letting an application run on a system. Some hackers or viruses attack the operating system and initially slow down the speed of the compromised computer. Later, the damage increase to the extent that the computer's hard disk might crash. Many hackers wish to gain control of a home computer and use it as an intermediary for launching attacks on Web sites, such as those of governments, banks, or financial systems. In these cases users' computers become tools for perpetrating cyber crime.

Securing Your Home Network

Initially, many individuals and small businesses ignored the fact that there were potential threats to their home computers. However, as more and more people accessed the Internet, they realized the threat is not only real, it is growing daily. These days, home computers are often the most vulnerable targets. The people who use computers at home are generally not very alert for security threats and are not as inclined to formalize a security plan as would a small business owner, who relies on a computer and the data on it for his or her livelihood. Users must be aware of the potential challenges their home networks have on the security front. Intruders might easily break into a system to get credit card numbers, bank account numbers, and Internet banking passwords to deplete victims' accounts. The monetary information in a computer system is not the only thing these hackers want. They can use the space in victims' hard disks, central processing units, and the same Internet connection. Though a broadband connection is more likely to be a target due to its high speed, it does not mean intruders will spare a dial-up connection.

Hackers try to target and use as many computers as possible. The more their network is spread, the more it will be difficult for cyber-crime experts to catch and stop the criminal.

Using an e-mail with a virus is the simplest way to intrude into a system. While reading the infected e-mail, users do not realize the virus has created a hidden entrance in their somewhat insecure system for the intruder's attack. The intruder installs new programs in the system that help him or her use the system for his or her purposes. These programs create several backdoors for future attacks so that the hacker can work on the system even if a user has plugged the initial entrance point.

E-mail is not the only means of receiving a virus or a Trojan horse. Users might get one from a chat or instant messenger as well. They might receive a virus through a sent file, with the virus hidden as an extension of a known file type. A common user would think the extension has an error and remove its unnecessary part to read the file. As soon as the extension is removed, the file with multiple viruses opens to damage the computer. The "LOVE-LETTER-FOR-YOU.TXT.vbs" virus is an example of this. When .vbs was removed from the extension to read the file, the virus contained in the file executed and delivered its malicious payload onto systems.

Securing Your Business Network

Small-business owners are a popular target for computer hackers and other malicious forms of attack. Many small-business owners believe they are too small to be a target. This laid-back attitude leads to insecure and improperly configured small-business networks that become easy targets to online threats. There have been many incidents in the past where small businesses have been the victim of attack, forcing them to shut down business for a week or more due to computer system failure or impact on the financial system, network operation, or Web site functionality. Owners must be prepared for and armed against the following potential threats to their small-business networks:

Spamming

Most small-business owners receive these unwanted commercial messages in their e-mail inboxes. Those who think it is not a threat should think again. Spam wastes time and bandwidth. If all the employees of a small business are receiving the same volume of spam, think of the total space it is occupying (if not deleted) and the total amount of time wasted dealing with spam. Moreover, these spam e-mails can be loaded with viruses.

E-mail spoofing

Spoofing is the term used when an e-mail comes from a different source than what it appears to be. These are generally used to lure the user to release sensitive information, such as a user name and/or password.

Phishing

Phishing has become the favorite trick of hackers these days. An e-mail might appear to have arrived from an official site, such as

Microsoft or eBay. When a recipient opens the link in the e-mail, it goes to real-looking, but fraudulent, Web site that will prompt the user to enter login or other crucial information. This information is then captured and used by the hacker to gain access to the victim's financial data, network, or secure online accounts.

Viruses

Viruses are small programs that replicate by themselves and cause harmful actions on an operating system. They are hidden in harmless-looking e-mails often referencing games and images. The topics of the e-mails are tempting enough to trick readers into opening them, executing the virus, and infecting their machines as the program attempts to replicate throughout a network.

Worms

Worms have the ability to replicate themselves just as viruses do. The only difference is that worms do not harm an operating system. Instead, they typically self replicate and consume bandwidth or create "backdoors," allowing unauthorized access to the system by an intruder.

Trojan horses

These are another set of malicious programs. They appear to be legitimate software installations, but contain hidden malicious software that typically allows access to sensitive data or remote access to the system by an intruder.

Spyware

This is a general term to describe any software that is designed to "spy" on a computer or network. These programs track user activity and often transmit it to an unauthorized recipient.

Tampering

When packets of data or information travel from a computer to others, the information and the data contained in those packets can be intercepted, partially deleted, or altered.

Information disclosure

Disclosure of crucial information to someone who is not supposed to have access to it can lead to potential harm to a home or business.

If the network security of a business is intact, computer systems are protected from most online threats. The installation of antivirus software, antimalware, and reputable firewalls can prevent the majority of attacks from occurring or from inflicting significant damage. Securing computer networks from attack will minimize network disruptions. When critical home and business financial and other data is safe and secure, users will have peace of mind and minimize exposure to fraud and malicious attack.

Security in Windows XP Networks

Those using the Windows XP operating system for their home or business computers must know how to make all systems secure using the following security features:

- **NTFS file system**: The NTFS file system feature allows users to set permissions to the file level, making it safer and faster than the previous file systems, such as FAT32. FAT32 is the file allocation table used in older versions of Windows, such as Windows 98 and Windows Me.

- **Disabling simple file sharing:** Windows XP Professional edition has the ability to disable simple file sharing, making it difficult for someone to steal the data in files because the system requires user authentication before accessing shared folders. This feature is not available in XP Home edition. Those using the NTFS file system need to go to the folder properties and choose the option "Make this folder private."

- **Passwords for users of all accounts**: To make a system secure, Windows XP can assign individual passwords for all user accounts. Users can leave the password blank; however, users will not be able to remotely access the system over the network.

- **Restricted administrative rights**: Usually, home and many small business users give administrative rights to all of their user accounts. This exposes a system to greater risk from hackers and internal sabotage. It is better to give administrative rights to just one or two user accounts and restrict access to most others.

- **Disabling of guest account**: Guest accounts, if enabled, provide an easy path into a system for hackers. In Windows XP, users can disable the guest account. The guest account option can be removed from the Fast User Switching welcome screen as well as the local logon menu.

- **Firewall**: The more computers stay connected to the Internet and the higher the speed of a network's broadband, the more users are at risk. Windows XP has a built-in firewall to restrict and filter the incoming traffic without restricting outgoing traffic. It is better than nothing, but users should consider a much stronger firewall application from a third-party provider.

- **Internet connection sharing (ICS)**: With the Internet connection sharing feature in Windows XP, one user can be connected to the Internet and the rest of the users can share the connection. It is good for small-office or home purposes. At the same time, this is risky because all the systems can be affected when attacked through the Internet; therefore, it is better to use a hardware router or network hub.

- **Automatic updates**: Automatic updates help the system patch up any system flaws or known exposures to avoid attack when connected to the Internet. When the system is not updated against the latest threats, the system is at the highest risk. This of course includes updates to antivirus software and antimalware installed on a system.

- **Security of wireless networks**: Chapter 10 is dedicated to wireless networks; however, wireless networks must be secured to protect against hacking attempts and illegal access. You can have a completely insecure wireless network, which allows anyone to join your network and access your computer, files, peripherals, and Internet connection without your knowledge or permission.

- **Security of backups**: With all the above security features in place, do not forget to perform full system backups and secure those backups in a safe location: an external hard drive, online storage account, or other third-party backup solution, such as Carbonite (**www.carbonite.com**). Users also need to keep the emergency repair/startup disks properly locked up and away from workstations.

Security in Windows Vista Networks

Microsoft has added several new security features in Windows Vista networks to make them safer and more secure. The following are the new key security features of a Windows Vista network:

- **User account control**: User account control is a new feature in Windows Vista that treats all the users in the same standard mode. This even includes the administrator. For administrative functions, like installing new software or changing the settings of the system, the system gives prompts to the user. This feature also prevents spoofing the user identity. When the system starts, it asks for user ID and password in the secure mode; until the credentials are provided, the screen is temporarily disabled.

- **BitLocker Drive Encryption**: BitLocker drive encryption encrypts the full disk; therefore, the data is secure from unauthorized access.

- **Windows firewall**: The firewall in Windows Vista offers some new benefits, such as outbound packet filtering to check for viruses and spyware and a management console that enables remote administration. Outbound packet filtering is used to stop malware from stealing sensitive information off a computer and transmitting it across the Internet. This improvement in Vista eliminates one of the major weaknesses in the Windows XP firewall.

- **Windows Defender**: Windows Defender is an antispyware utility that checks the entry of any spyware in the system and monitors any kind of changes that might be caused due to a spyware attack.

- **Parental controls**: Parental controls are based on user account control. Children's accounts can be blocked for content such as drugs, Web e-mail, Web chat, and pornography. It is also possible to limit the amount of time children can use the system or access the Internet.

- **Encrypting file system**: This is a feature that lets you store data on your computer hard drive in an encrypted format.

- **Preventing exploits**: This feature provides address space layout randomization, which might load critical system files at any of the 256 locations in the memory at random locations versus specific locations. Because the system file location is random in any of 256 locations, it is much more difficult for malicious code to find the crucial system files.

- **Data execution prevention**: Data execution preventing is present in some processors. It flags some part of the memory as containing data instead of executable codes. This leads to no arbitration errors and therefore no overflow errors.

- **Digital rights management**: Digital rights management helps digital content providers and corporations protect copyright data from being copied. This includes content such as DVDs and Blu-ray discs.

- **Authentication and logon**: Credential providers have replaced the interactive logon and authentication in previous versions when logging into computers and network. You can now use biometric devices, smart cards, and PINs for computer and network access.

- **Network-access protection**: Through network-access protection, Vista makes sure the system that is connected to any network is trusted and approved by the network administrator.

Security in Windows 7 Networks

Microsoft Windows 7 has the following security features to save home or small-business systems from various threats:

- **BitLocker**: The encryption technique for the security of the operating system has been carried forward from Vista with some improvements. In Windows 7, BitLocker automatically encrypts new data when it is running, so it is seamless to the end-user, providing maximum protection.

- **BitLocker To Go**: BitLocker To Go allows even the external hard drives and USB drives to be encrypted. Thus, the security strings are tight even around the portable drives.

- **Action Center**: The Action Center was called Security Center in previous versions of Microsoft Windows. The name has changed with some improvements. It not only helps in securing the operating system, it also ensures the data is in place if the system crashes by chance.

- **User account control**: User account controls in Windows 7 are the same as in Vista. However, in Vista, users can easily ignore the warning. In Windows 7, this feature was customized and personalized to an extent that the user become conscious of what is happening to his or her computer.

- **DirectAccess**: DirectAccess is for businesses that need to connect to a virtual private network. The process of connecting through a VPN has been streamlined, and therefore, there is no data leakage during transmission.

- **Biometrics**: Biometric drives and Windows 7 software are compatible for third-party developers to use in their own software. This remarkably improves the security of the system and the network.

- **AppLocker**: AppLocker also has descended from Vista. It gives the administrator the right to decide which user can use which applications. The administrator can even restrict the scripts and programs that can be run by certain users.

- **Windows filtering platform**: Windows filtering platform was initially introduced in Vista. With Windows 7, third-party developers can use the Windows firewall in their software. It means the Windows firewall can also coexist with the firewall of a third-party developer. The user can choose to use either or both the firewalls at the same time;

therefore, no unwanted user can fiddle with the firewall to get access to a certain program.

- **Windows firewall**: The Windows firewall has also been updated in Windows 7. In this, users can choose the intensity of firewall protection, depending on their location. They can choose a more intense protection when they are in a public area than when at home.

How are Windows 7 Networking and Network Security Improved?

Windows 7 is without a doubt the most secure and stable version of Windows ever produced. Here is a look at some other improvements in the security and networking features of Windows 7 versus other operating systems:

- Windows 7 supports more than one firewall. The use of a third-party firewall along with the Windows firewall helps you receive the benefits of both.

- Encrypting of external hard drives makes the process of data transferring through an external hard drive safer than ever before.

- With the new Windows Biometric Framework, third-party developers can use biometric devices such as a finger print in their own software, leading to more secured networks and systems. The reader configuration has also been made easy. One can easily store fingerprint data and control the process of logging into the system.

- DirectAccess provides secured connection through VPNs.

- User account control has been made more personalized and therefore user friendly.

- The new system-restore includes a list of programs deleted and added by the user. It provides more information to the user before he or she decides to restore a program.

Thus, it is not just the look and feel that has improved in Windows 7. The security-related features are also improved significantly over previous version. Of course, despite these advances, users must have current, updated antivirus, antimalware, and antispam software running to protect their computers and networks, as well as ensure they have optimized the security settings in Windows and installed all the latest patches and updates.

How to Test Your Network for Security Weaknesses

A common user question is "How do I test my network to see if it is secure?" The following are some of the questions and risks associated with each topic that help to determine the security status of a network:

Q. How many computers are connected to the Internet without a firewall in between?
The higher the number of computers without a firewall, the more porous and open for exploitation a system.

Q. What type of password enforcement are you using?
Weak passwords of user accounts can facilitate the hacking of a network.

Q. What type of administrator password enforcement are you using?
Weak administrative passwords can lead to handing over administrative control of computers and networks to a hacker.

Q. Are there any missing operating system patches on any of the computers?
Missing patches make computers more porous for virus and worm attacks.

Q. How many network ports are left open on various workstations and how many of these ports can be considered risky?
The higher the number of open ports, the higher the number of vulnerable computers in a network.

Q. Are each of the business applications checked for security defects and how frequently are they checked for such defects and patches/upgrades?
A negative answer shows weaker application security.

Q. Does the system have an active data-backup program?
In the case of a malicious attack, virus, or data loss, users must have a reliable data backup from which to restore information.

Q. Are computes running updated antivirus, antimalware, antispam, and other antispyware defense programs?
Users must install a comprehensive defensive suite against all known threats.

These are just basic pointers to help users gauge network vulnerability against any kind of threat from the Net. There are several vulnerability assessment tools available to help users assess the weakness of a network and there are companies that specialize in network security and can assist in properly configuring a network against attack. Online threat scanners can assist in properly configuring a network against attack. Online threat scanners can quickly identify known threats, viruses, worms, Trojan horses, and more. Most vulnerability assessment tools can sweep for firewall configuration weaknesses, open ports, known exploits, weak access control policy, and improper configuration of applications that might lead to network security violations.

Hacking into a Network

Hacking a network is the process of accessing and making changes in a network without authorization. On a positive note, it is often done to check the weaknesses of a network so users can ensure they are fully protected against a malicious attack. On a negative note, it is used to gain illegitimate access to a network without the permission of the owner and to use it for one's selfish interest or cause damage, destruction, or data theft. The following are the basic steps a professional hacker would take to hack into a network:

Target a network

Before hacking into a network, it is important to find a target network to launch an attack. The hacker would require some information, such as network address range, host names, exposed hosts and applications exposed on them, versions of the operating system and the applications in use, the host's and applications' state of patching, the structure of the applications, and structure of the backup server.

Range of network address and host names

The hacker would like to know the locations of the target network. Hackers would start looking at the various networks registered on a particular site at any point in time. They would try to collect any information regarding the target network from that particular site. An extranet or a business partner with poor security can be a favorable target. Then, the attacker looks for host names. On a large network, he or she would try nslookup, a Web-based DNS Lookup request. A Domain Name System (DNS) lookup will reveal the IP address of a domain name. There are many sites that let you perform DNS lookups, such as **www.zoneedit.com/ lookup.html**. You can also perform reverse DNS lookup with an IP address to get the associated domain names. A DNS is a machine that stores and translates an assigned IP address to the corresponding domain name. This lets you look up a Web site such as **www.atlantic-pub.com** by the domain name, which is easy to remember, compared to the numerical IP address, or in this case 216.82.97.105, which would be very difficult to remember.

Or, the hacker might opt for zone transfer, a DNS server that is improperly configured allowing anyone to query and obtain a DNS listing — all the DNS records associated with a particular domain — for a certain domain. In the case of zone transfer, the attacker would request a copy of the DMZ zone — the portion of a Domain Name System that has administrative responsibilities — to the DNS server, replicating the databases containing the DNS data across a set of DNS servers. If a hacker gains a copy of the entire DNS zone, he or she now has a listing of all hosts in that domain, simplifying the hacking process.

Easy targets and exposed applications

If a target is exposed, the hacker might not need any tool to hack that network. The only thing required is that Internet Control Message Protocol (ICMP) traffic is kept running. ICMP is an error reporting and diagnostic tool. The IP address should be changed to find an appropriate one in the target range. Then, the hacker keeps sending the ICMP echo to each of the hosts on the target network. The hacker might use a port scanner to check if the host is listening or not (if the connection is made or not). If the host is listening, the connection becomes complete and the port scanner will inform the same to the hacker. The port scanner might also inform the hacker about the various applications exposed on the host. Some of the favorable applications for hacking are FTP clients and FTP servers, HTTP servers, and Telnet mail servers. All of these are used on the Web for server administration, serving Web pages to client browsers and file transfers.

Information regarding the versions of operating system and patch state

The version of a Web application on the host server is important information. There are certain applications — such as Standard Mail Transfer Protocol (SMTP) and Post Office Protocol (POP), which are used to handle e-mail traffic on the Internet and other Web servers — that display a banner when someone tries to connect to a network. This banner is an indication for the hacker that tells him or her the version that the server is running. Information regarding the patch state is another interesting and useful piece of information to the hacker. This reveals the vulnerability of the application. A vulnerability scanner can also be of use to check which part of the application is open.

Structure of applications and back-end servers

It is difficult to get this information. However, if the hacker is lucky enough, he or she will be able to exploit them better and faster.

Elevating privileges

The first step to cracking a network is to send commands to the target network for becoming an internal user on one of the systems to be able to use the privileges of an internal user. Because the hacker cannot directly connect to the database, he or she sets up a listener on the external network. With the use of trivial file transfer protocol (TFTP), a very basic form of File Transfer Protocol (FTP), a hacking tool such as Netcat can be installed in the operating system of the target. Netcat creates a socket to pipe the commands of the hacker into the system, and he or she gets the foothold into the network to become a privileged user.

Gaining command over the domain name

After getting control over the database server and the Web browser, the hacker's next step is take ownership and control of the domain name. The hacker might attack directly to gain command over the domain name. If it fails, a Trojan horse can be used to get any of the users do the same for the hacker. If that too fails, the hacker might try a passive attack. Once controlled, domain name records might be altered and directed to fraudulent Web sites and mail servers.

This is the general procedure a hacker uses to hack into a network. It is just a general guide of the overall process, so that readers can defend their own computers and networks from being victims of hacking attempts.

Advanced Network Monitoring and Protection

With the increase of cyber crimes throughout the Internet, companies are looking for more advanced tools to monitor and protect their networks. There are several companies that offer network monitoring and protection services against the latest threats. These services include management of the following:

- **Firewall**: A firewall is the basic necessity for securing a network if it is connected to the Internet. Monitored firewall service providers can remotely manage a firewall to safeguard both the hardware and the software in a network.

- **Intrusion detection systems**: This service includes detection of any kind of intrusion to a network, system, service, or data. The network-based monitors usually match the activity against the profiles of various known attacks.

- **IP-VPNs**: In comparison to intranets and extranets, virtual private networks (VPNs) are secure private connections. Management of VPNs by network-monitoring firms reduces security threats by ensuring maximum-security procedures are implemented. An intranet is a private network contained within an enterprise network. Access to an intranet is not allowed from outside the network except through the use of VPNs, which allow validated users to establish sessions that grant access through firewalls to an intranet. An extranet is very similar to an intranet except that an extranet extends a corporate intranet to include external access, such as business partners, vendors, suppliers, and more. An extranet does not allow public access to a corporate intranet, but does allow some external access for validated users.

- **Antivirus protection**: Antivirus protection is another basic requirement. This checks for viruses at the firewall, in e-mails, in attachments to e-mails, and during all file transfers.

- **Endpoint threat protection**: Endpoint devices, such as desktop computers or servers, are detected and protected against any kind of irregularities.

- **Authentication**: If a user tries to access any system or applications, authentication management service gives directions to processes for the verification of that user.

- **Content filtering**: Depending on the security policy, unsuitable content is isolated and blocked from being accessed by any users.

- **Vulnerability assessment**: This involves checking all computer and network systems for any security risk, weakness, or threat. It includes assessment of the network, operating system, as well as applications.

This list includes the points now considered as advanced tools for network monitoring and protection. However, with new challenges coming up each day, these tools need to be continuously upgraded and improved to meet them.

This chapter was presented as a crash course into basic network security. For larger and more complex networks, which use servers, domain name controllers, Web servers, and exchange servers, users should employ a professional networking consultant to ensure their networks are optimized for performance, efficiency, and security.

CHAPTER 10

Wireless Network Security: How to Secure Your Wireless Network

This chapter deals entirely with wireless networks, how they work, and how to encrypt and secure a wireless network. It gives users some basic knowledge of wireless network hacking techniques so they can defend their home or business wireless networks. This chapter will provide you with a comprehensive guide to wireless network security so you can protect your network against intruders.

These days, wireless networks are common. They are used in coffee shops, restaurants, hotels, public spaces, airports, and in homes and businesses. Wireless networks are ideal for the home and small business environment, but users must take steps to ensure their wireless networks are secure and protected. One can scan wireless networks in a community and find many that are completely unprotected. This means that anyone can join those wireless networks and gain access to their Internet connections, as well as potentially gain access to the connected devices, printers, drives, and more. The use of small business and home wireless networks has exploded in recent years, primarily due to convenience, relatively low cost, and fairly simple installation. The proliferation of wireless devices such as routers, netbooks, and network-capable gaming consoles has resulted in a significant increase in the number of homes and businesses equipped with wireless networks.

Before going into the details of wireless networks, users must devote some time to understanding the basics of what a network is, how it works, and what users intend to accomplish when establishing a network.

A computer network is simply a group of two or more computers or devices connected so they might communicate with each other. A computer network can be wired or wireless and is usually built with a combination of different types of hardware and software, such as routers, hubs, switches, or repeaters. Computer networks are immensely popular and have a wide range of applications and uses. Some basic purposes for networks are:

- **Communication**: Particularly in small businesses, colleges, or home networks. This lets all the individual computers connect, allowing communication and sharing of information.

- **Resource sharing**: Resources such as TVs, gaming systems, scanners, printers, and Internet connections can be used by any computer on the network without being directly connected to it.

- **File sharing**: A network makes it possible for everyone on a common network to access files anywhere on the network. Ideal for sharing work documents, photographs, videos, and more.

- **Remote access**: Having a network allows greater mobility and helps facilitate remote access to the network computers while traveling.

- **Data backup**: A network can also help maintain a backup of certain important documents on several computers in the network by using shared storage or network storage devices to consolidate and improve data backup speed and integrity.

A computer network can be classified in a number of ways. Several classification metrics are:

- **Connection methodology**: Connection methodology takes into account the type of hardware and software used to establish the communication channel between computers within a network. Connection methodologies are broadly categorized in:

    - **Wired technologies**: These include fiber optics, twisted pair wires, and coaxial wires. Most home and business networks use Cat V twisted pair network cables, and most computers are built with Cat V network receptacles. Coaxial cable carry signals for traditional cable TV. Fiber optics is growing in popularity due to its speed and is used by Verizon for its home and business Fiber Optic Service (FiOS). Fiber optics is approximately 1,000 times faster than twisted pair and 90 times faster than coaxial wires.

- **Wireless technologies**: This technology is implemented via cellular and personal communication service (PCS) systems, Bluetooth, wireless Web, terrestrial microwave, communications satellites, and wireless LANs. PCS is the name for the 900-MHz radio band used for digital mobile phone services in the United States.

- **Physical distance or scale**: Networks can be classified as private networks, local area networks (LANs), wide area networks (WANs), intranets, extranets, and the Internet.

- **Relationship**: Every computer in the computer network might be assigned a function according to the relationship between them. For example: client-server or peer-to-peer.

  - **Client-server:** In this case the client initiates the communication and requests any service from the server and the server is a host and shares resources with its client.

  - **Peer-to-peer (P2P)**: A P2P system has no particular infrastructure. All participants offer limited resource sharing. This is the type of network you would build in the typical home or small office environment with Windows XP, Windows Vista, or Windows 7.

For discussing any computer network, having a slight insight in the computer network architecture is very handy. Although capabilities, prices, and equipment features are changing drastically with the rapid advancement of technology, the essential network functions they perform are still very much the same. The main components of any data-transmission system are a transmitter and a receiver. The communication link is the physical path between the transmitter and the receiver. The physical layer is responsible to transmit raw bits over a physical link between any two network nodes. Transmission media can be classified as:

- Guided
- Nonguided

It should be noted that in either case, the communication is in the form of electromagnetic waves. With guided media, the waves are guided through a solid medium, such as copper twisted pair wires, copper coaxial cables, or fiber optics, which have increasingly gained importance due to their high-speed capacity. In unguided media, the electromagnetic waves are transmitted into the atmosphere. In guided media, the signal to be transmitted is confined to the solid medium that is used for transmission purpose. In unguided mediums, various factors affect how far the signal is broadcast, including temperature, humidity, physical barriers, and the strength of the broadcast. This is why users might detect their neighbors' wireless signals but they are typically low in overall strength.

Wireless communication is not a new idea. Today, it is said that the future for communication is wireless or fiber optics. All nonmobile devices will use fiber optics and all mobile devices will use wireless. With the successful venture of the first handheld computers (laptops), the idea of connecting them to the Internet in a wireless environment was born. Work on wireless connectivity was stimulated with the fast pace of technology development. Internet technology has made surprising strides. Wireless networking gives users freedom from cumbersome wires and it makes laptops and other handheld devices more portable than ever. By installing a credit card-sized PC card in a notebook (most of them have built in wireless networking capability), users can efficiently send and receive data at a high rate, to anywhere on Earth. With wireless it is possible to get up-to-date news, entertainment, sports, e-mail, and more from virtually anywhere. Broadband "air cards" enable high-speed connectivity from virtually anywhere there is a cellular signal.

A wireless network is defined as a network in which two or more computers or devices are connected to each other for communication, without the use of any wires. A simple example of a wireless network is a cellular network, which consists of a huge number of wireless subscribers who have telephones that can be used on the move. A home network might consist of a computer with a cable modem and a router. The router, which broadcasts a wireless signal, will allow computers, printers, and gaming devices to connect with each other forming a wireless network and sharing Internet access. Wireless technology continues to improve as technology advances and the cost of wireless products continues to decrease.

Wireless networks can be classified into the following categories, on the basis of distance and scale:

- Wireless personal area networks (PANs)
- Wireless local area networks (WLANs)
- Wireless wide area networks (WANs)
- Cellular device networks

The following sections discuss each of these classifications in depth and how technology used for wireless communication changes with distance.

Wireless PANs

A personal area network (PAN) is a network that is used for data transfer in a very short range. The interconnecting devices are centered on an individual person's workspace. All devices, such as wireless keyboards or Bluetooth mice, are connected in a wireless way. Wireless personal area networks typically use Bluetooth or infrared technology.

Wireless LANs

In simplest terms, a wireless LAN is a local area network in which mobile users can connect via radio or any other wireless media. Wireless LANs are becoming increasingly popular in business and home use today. A home wireless network is a WLAN. The need to collaborate and share up-to-date information without the hassles of cables has paved the way for wireless LANs. Most home and small-business wireless networks are peer-to-peer, meaning there is no client-server relationship. All "peers" are equal members of the network; none provide traditional "server" operations or services.

Users should note that an intranet is a private and a much more secure version of the public Internet. Intranets enable employees to access official databases and have access to corporate information and applications. They are typically available over a TCP/IP network through a Web browser. These resources reside on local servers usually. People can use the company resources by logging on to the company's network. To make the system secure, the system is provided by an authentication system.

These are the prominent technologies used as a solution to wireless LANs:

- **Spread spectrum**: Spread spectrum is a wideband radio frequency technique, usually used by the military for secure, reliable communication for critical missions.

- **Infrared**: Infrared technology is occasionally used in LANs. High-performance directed infrared is impractical for mobile users and therefore is used only to implement fixed subnetworks. Infrared technology lets two devices share and exchange information wirelessly through infrared ports. Because this is for short-range use only, it is not practical for most applications.

Wireless WANs

Local area networks usually have a limited range. To extend the range of LANs, wireless is employed, particularly when cabling is costly or difficult. For these purposes wireless bridges — wireless routers — are used to extend data communications between buildings. This is made possible by directional antennas at each end and a clear line of site between locations. The technology employed includes microwaves, lasers, and spread spectrum.

Wireless Technologies

Most notebook computers and personal digital assistants (PDAs) have infrared (IR) ports. Major mobile phone brands have at least one infrared-enabled handset and even wristwatches are beginning to incorporate infrared data ports. Infrared technology is used to implement a wireless interface to connect laptops and other portable machines to a desktop computer equipped with an IR transceiver.

Bluetooth is an omnidirectional wireless technology, meaning it can communicate with many devices at one time. The technology in Bluetooth wirelessly links cell phones, computers, headsets, computer hardware, and many other devices over short distances.

Terrestrial microwave technology consists of dish antennas about 3 meters (about 10 feet) in circumference. They are mounted to achieve line-of-sight transmission to receiving antennas. Microwaves are primarily used in long-haul telecom services as an alternative to fiber optics. They are also used for television and voice transmission.

Wireless Application Protocol (WAP) is a technology that allows you to access the Web as well as Web-based applications. It also allows you to conduct electronic commerce via electronic devices, such as PDAs.

Wi-Fi stands for wireless fidelity. Wi-Fi, or wireless networks, are very effective in letting you deploy networks in areas that are difficult or impossible to hard wire, such as historical buildings and outdoor areas, and of course, Wi-Fi is widely used for public places such as libraries, hotel lobbies, Internet cafés, and other similar places. Wireless networks are the most common form of network deployed in homes as well. Computer users will find products supporting a wide range of wireless standards, including 802.11a, 802.11b, 802.11g, and 802.11n. Additionally, Bluetooth and various other non-Wi-Fi technologies also exist, each designed for specific networking applications.

The Institute of Electrical and Electronics Engineers (IEEE) created the first wireless standard, called 802.11. A wireless standard was created to standardize wireless technology to make manufacturers build components that are compatible with the established standard. Without this standard, there could be widespread incompatibilities between hardware. For example, your laptop might not be able to connect to a wireless network that is not based on the wireless standard. Multiple versions were introduced after the original to provide more bandwidth or prevent the signals from interfering with other technology.

Bluetooth, as discussed previously is a slightly different communications technology than the 802.11 standard. Bluetooth is only very short range and uses a low bandwith that saves power yet allows for excellent connections between devices in close proximity (for example, Bluetooth headsets or Bluetooth mouse).

WiMAX is yet another standard, commonly known as IEEE 802.16, which is used primarily for very large wireless networks, such as "metropolitan area networks." WiMAX is very impressive and can provide high-speed (broadband) wireless access for distances up to 30 miles, compared to the 802.11 standards, which can only reach about 300 feet. WiMAX has been deployed for projects that offer free or low-cost wireless Internet access across an entire city.

Wireless Security

Security in wireless networks is far more crucial than wired networks. Data to be transmitted within a wireless LAN is broadcast on radio frequencies, so that anyone within the range can intercept and interpret the data. Confidential information of a business, credit records, and customer information is all very sensitive data that must be protected.

As the technology improves, hackers are also becoming more intelligent and innovative. Being a part of a mobile network is fantastic; however, it is obvious hackers find wireless networks relatively easy to break into. Hackers even employ wireless technology to break into wired networks. Hacking methods have become much more refined and better; therefore, users need to provide sufficient measures for the protection of data to use the wireless transmission for critical data. Today, wireless communication is becoming more central in telecommunications, so wireless security becomes an important issue. IEEE 802 standards have implemented certain security measures to protect data.

Before they take any measures for securing their wireless networks, users must identify the threats a wireless system can experience. Major threats usually affect the following aspects:

Security of the Physical System

A wireless system is made of a number of physical devices such as the access points, transmitters, and receivers. These can be attacked by an intruder. Stealing an access point is one of the simplest attacks. If any unwanted party happens to break in to a system and use services and information reserved for authorized users, it is called unauthorized access.

Privacy

In an attack on your privacy, an unwanted party accesses the data-communication channel and gets information that is owned by a person or business. Unwanted parties can be either enemies or competitors.

Security is an important issue in both wired and wireless networks. A network can be attacked in several different ways. Any attack on a network can be classified as:

Active attack

Active attacks are easily detected because users can find the active role of intruders between the communication links; however, they are difficult to prevent.

Passive attack

Passive attacks are snooping or eavesdropping. The goal is to access information that has been transmitted. These kinds of attacks are difficult to detect.

Due to the agility of wireless networks they are more vulnerable. The following section will further discuss the kinds of attacks a wireless network might experience.

Brute-force attacks on physical devices

One of the simplest attacks is an attack on the devices in the wireless network. The cracker reconfigures the devices (particularly the access point) with fake configurations and commands. Such reconfigurations can also affect routers, switches, and intelligent hubs. A whole network can be brought down in this manner. In these cases the solution is either to reboot or to reconfigure all the devices in the network.

Fake reply

Data is sent in packets or units on a communication link. In this type of attack, the hackers capture the data packet transmitted and subsequently retransmit it to construct unwanted access.

Modification

Suppose you need to send a message to your friends: "I will meet you at the restaurant at 5 p.m." The unauthorized user captures the information and changes it to his or her benefit. In large organizations such modification can be fatal. This is often called the "man-in-the middle" attack.

Release of message content

In a release of message content attack the attackers do not bother to make a smooth transmission, instead they aim to access e-mails or any files being transferred.

Traffic analysis

In a traffic analysis attack, the attacker's goal is to identify the location of the receiver and transmitter. They might also be interested in finding out the frequency at which the data transfer is being carried out and also the length of the message and the technique that is being employed on the packet of messages to make them secure, such as encryption methodology. Such information can easily tell the intruders the nature of the data transmission.

Masquerade

Suppose you are an authenticated user and your wireless network is protected. You place a valid authentication sequence and the system logs you in. Later an unwanted party collects your authentication and replays it. This is an example of a masquerade, when a hacker is disguised as a legitimate user.

Interruption in services

In an interruption in services attack unauthorized people use the facilities restricted for the authorized users, reducing overall functionality or performance of a network.

Eavesdropping

Wireless networks are the most prone to these types of attacks. As data is transmitted over radio, anyone with a proper receiver can interpret the data. Also, devices that are capable of intruding upon a network and receiving data are very cheap to buy and easy to use.

Denial of service or jamming

Any attacker can use special equipment to produce the radio frequency over which data is being transmitted and use the equipment to overload the wireless network with extra, unwanted information, eventually degrading the system. Ultimately this results in network loss or denial of access for authorized users.

Identity theft or spoofing

With identity theft or spoofing, the intruders learn the MAC address of the devices being connected in the system and can use software to gain access to sensitive data, typically through spoofing a valid MAC address.

The caffé latte attack

This involves a hacker cracking the wireless encryption protocol (WEP) key from a remote wireless client and targeting the Windows wireless traffic by sending a flood of encrypted requests and gaining access to data. The name "Caffé Latte" was coined by hackers who determined that they could crack a WEP key in the time it takes you to drink a caffé latte coffee drink. As discussed previously, WEP is not the recommended wireless protocol.

There are some protection measures you can take to help defend against this and other similar attacks. When not in use, most laptops and Wi-Fi devices have an option to turn off the Wi-Fi signal; once it is off, there is no chance of hacking. As you use your laptop or wireless device, you keep adding new network locations to it, such as coffee shops, bookstores, hotels, or public forums. In most cases, you configure your laptop to automatically connect to these networks when they are in range; disabling this feature will ensure that your laptop does not automatically establish a wireless connection without your knowledge. Of course, ensure your system has the latest security patches and updates for maximum protection against known exploits and be cautious when connecting to non-secure wireless networks, because there are no encryption standards in place and your data can be easily intercepted.

Malicious connections

The goal of the hacker is simply to invade the client and the data in transit using network cards built in soft APs (laptops with special software) that pretend to be an access point on a network.

Besides all these types of attacks, users can expect attacks against encryption, improper configuration of access points, failure to enable security, and client-to-client attack by duplication of IPs.

Hacking a Wireless System

Users need to understand the weaknesses of different technologies of wireless communication. There are several distinct weaknesses or disadvantages to wireless networks such as broadcasting unlimited radio waves, broadcasting the service set identifier (SSID) so anyone can discover the network, and the variety of security protocols (WEP, WPA, etc). An SSID is a name that identifies a wireless network. This name is usually "broadcast" so wireless devices can find it. When you stay in a hotel and need to connect your laptop to its wireless network, you search for the SSID (network name) then connect to it. If you do not configure the network properly, hackers can easily access your wireless network. White hat hacking lets users identify the weakness of a network and the ways that intruders can hack into the system. It lets users know where they are vulnerable and how to improve security.

In simple terms, ISO 17799 is an information security code that covers a broad range of security issues and provides the best support for information security and in particular wireless security. ISO 17799 is an internationally accepted information security standard that is composed of two parts:

- Specification for information security management system
- Code of practice

Although this document does not provide any information on hacking itself, it can help users to identify areas vulnerable to hacking.

Wired equivalent protocol (WEP) is a set of algorithms to secure IEEE 802.11 wireless technology. It helps protect data in transit between the client devices and the access point (AP), via 64, 128, or 256-bit encryption, on a wireless link. In the networks that use 802.11 standards the data is transmitted over radio making detection and interdiction of data very easy. WEP was originally designed to provide users with protection equal to that of a wired network. WEP relies on a secret key that is shared between all the devices in a wireless system, including the AP. This key is used to encrypt message packets before they are transmitted. Encryption provides security to the message packets sent by the client. At the receiving end, an integrity check is carried out to ensure packets are not modified while they were transmitted. With WEP, it is nearly impossible to modify an encrypted message if the key has not been broken. Once data has been through the integrity test other measures must be taken to guarantee privacy. Such measures include:

- End-to-end encryption
- LAN security mechanisms, such as password protection
- Virtual Private Networks
- Authentication
- Client firewall software

WEP provides only 40-bit key encryption. Manufacturers have implemented their own extensions to WEP, to strengthen their wireless systems. Such methodologies include 104-bit keys and dynamic key management password protection. The encryption only provides protection up to a gateway because encryption happens at the link layer, not at the application layer. Therefore, every other wireless client who has the key can read the packets, because the key is shared across all clients. Thus, for public network access, WEP is not very effective. However, there are more secure protocols, such as WPA and WPA-PSK.

Some explanation of the differences between WEP, WPA, and WPA2 will help users understand why WPA2 provides stronger wireless security than WPA and WEP. WPA2 (also known as 802.11i) is the latest wireless standard. WPA significantly improved upon WEP security, and provides for a very secure connection that is also backwards compatible with most older wireless hardware. WEP (Wired Equivalent Privacy) is the oldest Wi-Fi protection standard and as discussed, it uses the same security key making it easy to break, especially with the wide variety of freeware designed to steal WEP keys. The reality is that a wireless network running WEP can be hacked quickly and easily by even the most basic hacker.

Wi-Fi Protected Access (WPA) was designed specifically to overcome the weaknesses of WEP. Most notably it included functionality to automatically change the encryption key for each data transmission, significantly improving security and reducing the ability to hack the signal and steal the encryption key. WPA uses TKIP (Temporal Key Integrity Protocol), an older technology, whereas WPA2 uses AES (Advanced Encryption Standard), which is even more secure than TKIP. The drawback of WPA2 is that you must have the hardware to support it. All modern wireless hardware supports WPA2; however, if you are using older routers and other wireless hardware, it may not support WPA2. You should always use WPA2 as your primary wireless security standard. If you cannot use this due to hardware, use WPA. The use of WEP is not recommended, because most hardware will at least support the WPA standard. With any wireless network, your weakest link is always going to be your password. A stronger password means a stronger encryption key, which reduces the chances of having your wireless network hacked.

Here are simple techniques used to attack WEP:

- **Cracking WEP Key**: Cracking a WEP Key is fairly simple. This can be easily accomplished with software programs such as WEP Attack, chopchop, WEPcrack, AirSnort, Air-Crack, and WEPlab.

- **Traffic Injection**: The attacker uses a passive means to find how a plain text message has been encrypted. They then use this knowledge to encrypt, packet and inject their own packets into the communication channel. Two such well-known tools for this are Airplay and WEPWedgie.

Securing Your Wireless System

It is important to conserve your data, protect its legitimacy, and keep sensitive information safe. Security provides protection against data thieves and network attackers who with time have become very powerful. Security attacks can target hardware, computers, or servers, and it can also attack the devices that make up a wireless system, such as routers. Organizations must take adequate measures and establish policies to define the importance of security.

The client in a wireless network must be protected. Security measures must not be so complicated that an average user cannot benefit from them; therefore, it is essential to understand the type of security hazards to a system and take appropriate protection measures. As previously mentioned, Wi-Fi protected access (WPA) is a type of security technology for wireless networks. The WPA pre-shared key (WPA-PSK) is the most common solution for a home or small business wireless network. It is easy to use and all modern routers support this security protocol. With WPA-PSK, users set up a "passphrase" or static key, just like they do with the older WEP system. However, WPA-PSK automatically changes the keys at preset intervals, which makes it significantly more difficult to hack. WPA-PSK is the ideal security protocol for any home or small business wireless network.

Users must be able to maintain confidentiality, integrity, and availability of data within their wireless networks.

- **Confidentiality**: Data must be incomprehensible to everyone except authorized users.

- **Integrity**: Data must be reliable and authentic.

- **Availability**: Data must be available to all authorized users.

Wireless security policy

Security is very important. So users' first steps must be to create a home or business policy that clearly lays out the definition of security and how to enforce it. It must specify that users cannot install unauthorized wireless systems and all the devices must be properly configured before being installed. It is critical to properly configure routers and other wireless devices to run in a secure, encrypted mode. Administrators must also change the user name and passwords for any wireless devices from their default user names and passwords. Using a port scanner tells users who is accessing a network and what applications are being used by the devices in the network. Sniffers and network analyzers help monitor a network and point out any malicious wireless equipment functioning in the network. Network analyzers tell users the status of a wireless network or if any unauthorized device is connected to the network. They can also help in tracking down the IP address and the traffic being transmitted from any malicious attack or unauthorized access.

A wireless intrusion-detection/prevention system (IDS/IPS) is another way of defending a system from denial of service attacks.

It is recommended that users employ a virtual private network (VPN). A VPN is a method that makes individual ports and network traffic secure in a wireless (or wired) network. Using a quality VPN software ensures that the traffic coming from the client end is secure. A VPN uses strong encryption to protect the data packets to make certain that the user's data, e-mail, and Web password are protected. If any client's link in the network is being sniffed or eavesdropped the strong encryption protects the data. It is nearly impossible for the data to be tapped. VPN client software helps to access a network from anywhere.

Difficult passwords help to ensure protection because they are difficult to remember and hard to guess. Security suites are the most reliable shield to monitor Internet traffic and at a minimum, systems should run antivirus and antispyware applications at all times.

Setting up Your Wireless Network

Although wired networks are reliable and relatively easy to set up, wireless networks can be more challenging. First, choose your wireless networking equipment. Here is a list of what users might need for a wireless network. In most cases users simply need a good router. A Wireless "N" Router, which is the latest and fastest standard, is recommended. 802.11G is a very common, fast, and reliable standard, and 802.11b is the oldest and slowest wireless standard. Most routers and network cards today are backwards compatible and designed for 801.11(N) or 802.11(g). Here are some other items users might need, depending on their wireless networks' needs:

- Network hub or switch: A switch is an intelligent hub that speeds up network traffic by smart forwarding message packets.

- Access point: An access point, or the base station, is very important to a wireless network. Access points connect various wireless devices to each other and these wireless devices to a wired network. They are available in consumer and commercial versions.

- Network router: A wireless router enables multiple computers to share a single Internet connection. For example, if you have a single Internet connection at your home and you and your brother want to share the same Internet from different computers, then you must get a router. Routers are easy to set up and broadcast powerful signals. When connected to cable, DSL, or fiber optics modems, they perform well and provide excellent wireless security when configured properly.

- Print server: A print server is used to add printers directly to the network instead of attaching a printer to each computer on the network. Many printers these days are network ready, meaning they can connect directly to a router port, or are wireless devices that can join a network like any other device.

- Wireless network interface adapter: A wireless network interface adapter is another very essential device. It connects a computer to a wireless network. Most laptops have wireless network adapters installed. It can be added to desktops through a desktop card or USB port.

Wireless Networking in Windows XP

When Windows XP was released in 2001, the idea of wireless was less popular and most computers still used wired network connections. However, provisions for wireless were made a part of Windows XP Service Pack 2 (SP2), enhanced with Windows Connect Now technology that made setting up wireless networks simple. It made it easier to create a new wireless network or add devices such as routers and printers to an existing wireless network.

There are three simple steps to set up a wireless network with Windows XP SP2:

- Connect the wireless router.
- Configure the wireless router.
- Connect the computer to the wireless network via wizard.

Windows XP (SP2) allows users to automatically detect wireless network signals in their vicinities. Users simply choose the networks they wish to connect to, enter the security code (if protected), and the IP address is negotiated, granting access to the network.

Wireless Networking in Windows Vista

Windows Vista was designed to keep the growing market of wireless networks more secure and reliable. Vista alerts users if they are connecting to an unprotected device and it will not connect users to ad-hoc networks automatically. Most importantly, Windows Vista supports WPA2, providing users with a high level of standard wireless security.

Vista has also taken noticeable measures for active and passive attacks.

Windows Vista computers can automatically connect to a system's internal wireless networks. When users run the network wizard, all the available wireless connection will be listed. To connect to a wireless network users simply open the start-menu, and select the "connect to" option, which opens the Network Wizard. Users then choose their wireless network, "click connect," and enter the security passphrase or key.

Wireless Networking in Windows 7

Window 7 allows users to access existing wireless networks in just one click. Windows Connect Now is the latest Microsoft technology designed to simplify wireless configuration. Simply connect to a router and Windows 7 completes all the necessary steps, including naming the network and turning on the router's security features. In Windows 7, users will see the wireless network icon in the bottom right hand corner of the screen. Simply click on it and a window will open with all available network connections. Users will see all VPN connections, and dial-up and wireless networks. Click on the desired wireless network to connect. Windows 7 will show the name of the network, strength of the signal, type of wireless security protocol, and the service set identifier (SSID). Enter the security key for the router and you are connected.

The Windows Network and Sharing center has significantly improved compared to the Vista version, providing users with a truly full-featured network control center that lets them connect to networks, diagnose problems, establish VPN connections, and share devices. In Windows 7, users can choose between home, work, and public settings, depending on the location of the network to which they are connected. A new feature in Windows 7 is the ability to set firewall settings based on which location the user is in, so that he or she can have customized preset settings to afford maximum protection.

HomeGroup is one of the best new features in Windows 7. Home-Group simplifies network sharing of files and printers on a home network. HomeGroup makes it easy to automatically share music, pictures, video, and document libraries with other computers in a home. HomeGroup is password protected and lets users decide exactly what is and what is not to be shared (Note: Windows 7 assigns this password to users; therefore, users must enter this unique password as they connect computers to the HomeGroup).

In previous versions of Windows, accessing files back and forth across a network was tedious and more often than not did not work. With HomeGroup, in one click users can move files across the network, pull files from other computers, and edit files on another computer, all quickly, easily, and most importantly in a very secure environment.

This chapter was designed to give users some information regarding wireless networks, how they work, and how to protect them. The key to safe wireless networking is to ensure a network is encrypted with a strong encryption protocol (such as WPA-PSK) and that the router user name and password have been reset to prevent unauthorized access at the router. Users should never run a wireless network in an unprotected mode, because this opens the network and computers up to exploitation and damage.

Users also should be sure to scan their wireless networks for unauthorized devices, such as other computers, which have joined the network and might be draining its resources. A great resource to monitor and manage networks is LANSPY, available for free at: **http://lantricks.com**. Overall, Windows 7 does a great job of providing users with excellent wireless security, as long as their routers are properly configured and they have encrypted their wireless signal with WEP, WPA, or WPA-PSK.

CHAPTER 11

Software Products to Protect Your Computers & Networks

There are dozens of software products to combat and defend against viruses, malware, spyware, and spam. These include blockers, firewall software, and network monitoring software. This chapter is not an endorsement or necessarily a review of any individual software products, but rather a compilation of recommended software applications that will protect computers and networks from malicious attacks. As mentioned in the introduction, this book provides information about free software applications as an alternative to commercially bought and subscription-based software when possible. All of the products in this chapter are reputable and perform exceptionally. This chapter will provide options, features, and product summaries. Pricing is not included because many of the listed products offer free trials and most offer discount pricing for multi-year subscriptions; however, if a product is free, that information is included. This chapter is intended to be a resource to help users choose which products are right for them.

Users can also read reviews of the latest software products at TopTenREVIEWS (**www.toptenreviews.com**). TopTenREVIEWS gives you the information and recommendations for the best product in a wide variety of categories using side-by-side comparison charts, news, articles, and videos. This is a terrific source for reviewing software products before you purchase them.

Internet Security Suites

An Internet security suite typically integrates most common security software into one bundle. Usually this includes antivirus, firewall, antispyware, and antiphishing elements, and might include other forms of malware protection. Internet security suites often include parental control software as well. None of the listed Internet security suites are free; most require subscriptions and annual subscription renewals. Most of the suites include licensing for up to three computers.

BitDefender Internet security

BitDefender (**www.bitdefender.com**) has two suite products entitled BitDefender Total Security and BitDefender Internet Security. Both have comprehensive antivirus, antiphishing, antispyware, antimalware, antispam, personal firewall, and privacy protection. They also both have Wi-Fi monitoring and parental controls. Total Security also features PC Tuneup, File Shredder, and backup functionality.

Kaspersky Internet Security

Kaspersky Internet Security (**http://usa.kaspersky.com**) features comprehensive antivirus, antiphishing, antispyware, antimalware, antispam, personal firewall, autorun disable, white listing (recognizing a set of trusted e-mails), and parental control features. It also includes a URL adviser to warn users of dangerous Web sites.

ZoneAlarm Internet Security

ZoneAlarm (**www.zonealarm.com**) features comprehensive antivirus, antiphishing, antispyware, antimalware, antispam, personal firewall, download protection, parental control, and credit bureau monitoring features.

Webroot Internet Security Essentials

Webroot Internet Security Essentials (**www.webroot.com**) features comprehensive antivirus, antiphishing, antispyware, antimalware, antispam, personal firewall, automatic backup, and privacy protection features.

BullGuard Internet Security

BullGuard's suite (**www.bullguard.com**) features comprehensive antivirus, antiphishing, antispyware, antimalware, antispam, personal firewall, and backup features.

TrendMicro

TrendMicro (**www.trendmicro.com**) has two suite products, Internet Security Pro and Internet Security. Both have comprehensive antivirus, antiphishing, antispyware, antimalware, antispam, and parental control features. Total Security also features added privacy and malware protection as well as backup functionality.

"Used with Permission from TrendMicro"

McAfee Total Protection

McAfee (**www.mcafee.com**) suite features comprehensive antivirus, antiphishing, antispyware, antimalware, antispam, personal firewall, backup, Web site safety rating, privacy protection, and home network protection features.

Norton Internet Security

Norton (**www.symantec.com**) features comprehensive antivirus, antiphishing, antispyware, antimalware, antispam, personal firewall, advanced privacy protection, and home network protection features. Norton also offers Norton 360, which has slightly different features, such as backup and PC tuneup.

AVG Internet Security 9.0

AVG Internet Security 9.0 (**www.avg.com**) features comprehensive antivirus, antiphishing, antispyware, antimalware, antispam, personal firewall, antirootkit, privacy protection and more.

Panda Internet Security

Panda Security (**www.pandasecurity.com**) features comprehensive antivirus, antiphishing, antispyware, antimalware, antispam, personal firewall, antirootkit, privacy protection, parental controls, and more. Panda also offers Panda Global Security. The main difference between the two products is that Panda Global Security features PC optimization and tuneup features. Panda Internet Security even lets users monitor network traffic. The following image is a screen shot from Panda Internet Security showing the main menu. At a glance you can monitor the status of antivirus, firewall, antispam, and other vulnerabilities, as well as ensure your product is up to date.

"Used with Permission from Panda Security"

The screen shot below shows the network monitoring capability of Panda Internet Security, a great feature for monitoring what is truly happening on your local network.

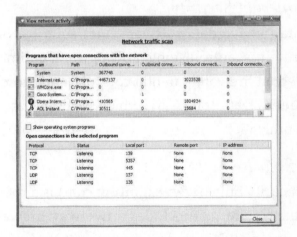

"Used with Permission from Panda Security"

Panda's Cloud Protection is a security solution specifically designed for small and medium-size businesses. Panda Security states that "Every Panda user is a sensor for new malware, sending statistical data about malware prevalence back to the cloud.

This new approach reduces bandwidth consumption on customers' PCs and provides faster and more comprehensive up-to-date protection. This innovative model not only allows detecting much more malware than the manual systems that some laboratories use, but is also able to detect even new threats not yet recognized. Combining Collective Intelligence and TruPrevent technologies, Panda is capable to detect the most sophisticated malware." Introduced in November 2009, users can find details on Cloud Protection here at **http://cloudprotection.pandasecurity.com.**

F-Secure Internet Security

F-Secure Internet Security (**www.f-secure.com**) features comprehensive antivirus, antiphishing, antispyware, antimalware, antispam, personal firewall, parental controls, and more.

G Data Internet Security

The G Data (**www.gdata-software.com**) suite features comprehensive antivirus, antiphishing, antispyware, antimalware, antispam, personal firewall, parental controls, and more. Other versions include G Data Total Care, which includes data backup and system optimization.

OutPost Security Suite

OutPost Security Suite (**www.agnitum.com**) is a robust, full-featured security suite that includes a two-way firewall, intrusion detection system (IDS), and Ethernet protection for automated defense against vulnerability probes and internal breaches. It also features a combined antivirus and antispyware scanner, host protection for proactively blocking unknown threats, antispam filter, Web and transaction security, and automated updates.

"Used with Permission from Agnitum, Ltd"

Antivirus Software

Although security suites provide users with a robust set of applications including firewalls, parental controls, network protection, and more, antivirus software simply concentrates on making sure a computer is protected against viruses, Trojans, worms, and other malware. More than half of the computers connected to the Internet today do not have antivirus software installed, or have expired or out-of-date software, providing minimal protection. Users must have active, updated antivirus software installed at all times. The good news is most modern antivirus software does much more than just prevent and destroy viruses, most offer advanced malware protection against a wide variety of threats. Most of the following antivirus solutions offer free trials and some are free.

Microsoft Security Essentials

Microsoft Security Essentials (**www.microsoft.com/Security_Essentials**) is free and nonintrusive. Unlike some other products, it is not resource-intensive on the central processing unit (CPU). Microsoft Security Essentials provides real-time protection against viruses, spyware, and other malicious software. It features comprehensive antivirus and malware protection and automatic updates.

A-squared Anti-Malware

A-squared Anti-Malware (**www.emsisoft.com**) offers comprehensive PC protection against Trojans, viruses, spyware, adware, worms, bots, keyloggers, rootkits, and dialers. A-squared Anti-Malware includes both malware and antivirus protection and uses two full-scan engines in the battle against malware. Users can also download a-squared free.

BitDefender Antivirus

BitDefender (**www.bitdefender.com**) features comprehensive antivirus and antimalware protection against viruses, spyware, phishing attacks, and identity theft. It also features automatic updates.

ZoneAlarm Antivirus

ZoneAlarm (**www.zonealarm.com**) features comprehensive antivirus and malware protection against viruses, spyware, and phishing attacks. It also contains a site status tool, OS firewall, and automatic updates.

Kaspersky Antivirus

Kaspersky (**http://usa.kaspersky.com**) features comprehensive protection against viruses, spyware, Trojans, worms, bots, and more. It also includes comprehensive phishing and identity theft defense and hourly automatic updates.

TrendMicro Antivirus + Anti-spyware

TrendMicro (**www.trendmicro.com**) software features protection against viruses, spyware, Trojans, worms, rootkits, bots, and more with active intrusion blocking.

McAfee VirusScan Plus

McAfee Virus Scan Plus (**www.mcafee.com**) features comprehensive antivirus and malware protection against viruses, spyware, and phishing attacks. It includes site status, built-in firewall, and automatic updates. This software comes with McAfee Active Protection technology and McAfee Site Adviser.

Norton Anti-Virus

Norton software (**www.symantec.com**) features comprehensive antivirus and malware protection against viruses and spyware, and a built-in firewall and automatic updates.

AVG Anti-Virus 9.0

AVG (**www.avg.com**) features comprehensive antivirus and malware protection against viruses and spyware. It includes a built-in firewall and automatic updates.

ESET Nod32 Antivirus 4

ESET (**www.eset.com**) features comprehensive antivirus and malware protection against viruses, spyware, and phishing attacks, and automatic updates.

F-Secure Anti-Virus

F-Secure Anti-Virus (**www.f-secure.com**) features comprehensive antivirus and malware protection against viruses, spyware, and phishing attacks, and automatic updates.

G Data Anti-Virus

G Data (**www.gdata-software.com**) features comprehensive antivirus and malware protection against viruses, spyware, and phishing attacks, and automatic updates.

Outpost Antivirus Pro

Outpost Antivirus Pro (**www.agnitum.com**) easily and effectively removes malware and viruses. The advanced host protection module protects users against new and unknown malware. It includes "ID Block" to protect personal information, including credit card data theft.

VIRUSfighter Pro

VIRUSfighter Pro (**www.spamfighter.com**) is a powerful antivirus program that does not drain a computer's resources. It offers protection against viruses and malware. Every time a new virus outbreak occurs, an effective antidote is quickly released and automatically installed. Updates are frequent, often several times a day. Individuals can try the program out for free for 30 days.

Cloud Antivirus

Cloud Antivirus (**www.cloudantivirus.com/en**) is Panda Security's free antivirus software. Rated by *PC Magazine* as the Editor's Choice as best free antivirus in detecting malware.

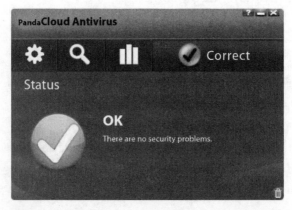

"Used with Permission from Panda Security"

Antispyware Software

Spyware and malware are prevalent on the Internet. Users must defend against spyware by using software effective in deterring, detecting, and removing spyware, keyloggers, and other malware. Many of the products in the Internet security suites and even some of the antivirus applications actively detect and deter spyware. This section will concentrate on software whose main purpose is to combat spyware.

Webroot Spy Sweeper

Webroot (**www.webroot.com**) offers one of the best antispyware and antimalware products on the market. Webroot's Spy Sweeper is award-winning, comprehensive, powerful, and highly effective. It includes automatic updates. Spy Sweeper is also available integrated into the Webroot Antivirus software.

CounterSpy

CounterSpy (**www.sunbeltsoftware.com**) is a powerful spyware and malware remover that is not resource intensive. It includes antimalware technology, kernel-level perpetual active protection, and boot-time scans to kill rootkits.

StopZilla

StopZilla (**www.is3.com**) is a powerful spyware and malware remover that removes and blocks spyware, adware, pop-up ads, phishing attacks, hijackers, rootkits, Trojans, bots, drive-by downloads, rogue programs, messenger service ads, keyloggers, malicious browser helper objects (BHO), dialers, and much more.

"Used with Permission from IS3, Inc."

Spyware Doctor

PC Magazine and *PCWorld* recommended Spyware Doctor (**www. pctools.com**) as a comprehensive antispyware and antimalware solution able to detect, remove, and block all types of spyware.

Ad-Aware

Ad-Aware (**www.lavasoft.com**) provides powerful protection against spyware, Trojans, rootkits, keyloggers, password stealers, adware, and more. There is a free version, though users can buy a more advanced, feature-rich version.

Malwarebytes

Malwarebytes (**www.malwarebytes.org**) is powerful software that protects against spyware and malware. Like Ad-Aware, it is free; however, users can buy a more advanced, feature-rich version.

Anti-Spy

Anti-Spy (**www.anti-spy.info**) software protects against spyware and malware. It detects and removes spyware, Trojans, keyloggers, and adware.

Spybot Search and Destroy

Spybot (**www.safer-networking.org**) is one of the most popular, free antispyware applications available.

SPYWAREfighter Pro

An easy to use antispyware program, SPYWAREfighter Pro (**www.spamfighter.com**) is guaranteed to protect against spyware and other threats to a computer.

Antispam Software

Many of the products, Internet security suites, and even some antivirus applications have built in antispam capabilities. Those will not be repeated in this section. Instead, the following entries will concentrate on software whose main purpose is to specifically combat spam.

Spam Agent

Spam Agent (**www.anti-spam-software.com**) includes more than 1,500 preset filters to blocks all unwanted spam and junk e-mail. It gives users the ability to create custom filters based on e-mail addresses, subjects, certain words, domains, and so on. It includes built-in functionality to report spammers and send abuse e-mails.

MailWasherFree

MailWasher (**www.mailwasher.net**) is free and never expires. It works with Outlook, Outlook Express, Incredimail, Thunderbird, Windows Mail, GMail, Hotmail, and other programs to effectively stop spam. MailWasher Pro is also available for purchase for multi-license or business use. MailWasher Pro allows you to preview multiple accounts and all aspects of your e-mail on the server before you download it to your computer, thus protecting you from spam, viruses, phishing attacks, and other nuisances. The program also learns what kind of e-mail you want to receive and adapts to your preferences. Other features help identify and protect you against viruses and worms. Also included are comprehensive, customizable filters, use of public blacklists to identify spammers, and multiple accounts.

SPAMfighter

SpamFighter (**www.spamfighter.com**) is absolutely free to use for home users. It works with Outlook, Outlook Express, Windows Mail, and Mozilla Thunderbird to automatically and efficiently filter spam and phishing fraud. SpamFighter Pro is also available for purchase for multi-license or business use.

IHateSpam

A superior spam filter, iHateSpam (**www.sunbeltsoftware.com**) delivers reliable e-mail security, blocking spam and filtering junk mail. Note: This product only works with Microsoft Outlook.

CloudMark Desktop

A superior spam filter delivering reliable e-mail security, Cloud-Mark Desktop (**www.cloudmark.com**) blocks spam and filters junk mail for Outlook, Outlook Express, and Thunderbird.

Vanquish

Vanquish (**www.vqme.com**) is a personal antispam filter for up to five POP mailboxes. It delivers reliable e-mail security, blocking spam and filtering junk mail.

Specialty Tools and Malware Protection

Microsoft Windows Malicious Software Removal Tool

The Microsoft Windows Malicious Software Removal Tool works on Windows 7, Windows Vista, Windows XP, Windows 2000, and Windows Server 2003. It checks for malicious software, removing any infections it finds. Microsoft releases an updated version of this tool on the second Tuesday of each month and as needed to respond to security incidents. Even if users do not have signs of malware, this is a useful tool to download and run. Users can download this tool at: **www.microsoft.com/security/malwareremove/default.aspx**.

Windows Live Safety Scanner

The Windows Live Safety Scanner is a free tool that scans a computer for malicious software. This scan will check for malware, viruses, and spyware, as well as check for vulnerabilities in an Internet connection. The Windows Live Safety Scanner can be found here: **http://onecare.live.com**.

NovaShield Anti-Malware

NovaShield (**www.novashield.com**) provides powerful protection against botnets, Trojans, keyloggers, rootkits, worms, and spyware.

A-squared Anti-Malware

A-squared (**www.emsisoft.com**) provides comprehensive PC protection against Trojans, viruses, spyware, adware, worms, bots, keyloggers, rootkits, and dialers. A-squared Anti-Malware includes both malware and antivirus protection and uses two full-scan engines in the battle against viruses, Trojans, backdoors, spyware, adware, worms, bots, keyloggers, dialers, and all other types of malware. Users can download a-squared.

Personal Firewall Software

A firewall is a security system for a computer and network. Firewalls control the traffic between a computer and the Internet, and control access to a computer or network from the Internet. A personal firewall protects a computer and network by blocking malicious attacks from hackers while still allowing users to perform their normal Internet activity. Firewalls will alert users in the event of any intrusion attempts and protect critical data from being accessed, stolen, or destroyed. Firewalls are often intimidating for novice users, but they are absolutely critical. Microsoft has made the decision to use a personal firewall very easy because they have been built firewalls into Windows XP, Windows Vista, and Windows 7 and activated them by default.

Firewalls protect systems from hackers and can also block malware. Any time a user connects a computer to the Internet, it is exposed and at risk. Hackers continually scan for exposed systems to exploit, damage, and destroy. Computers that run on the Internet with no firewall protection can quickly be exploited with malware and other hack attempts turning them into botnets quickly. You can lose control of your own computer and your own network. Internet security suites all come with personal firewalls. When installed, these will disable the built-in Windows firewall and replace it with their product. Computers only need one personal firewall at any time. Users should not install and activate more than one firewall at any time.

Personal firewalls are software, installed on each computer. Hardware routers are physical equipment that are typically connected between the modem or router and the computer connected to the Internet. There are some powerful, commercial hardware firewalls, but the following products are ideal for home or small business users.

In general, the use of wired routers, wireless routes, and broad-band gateways are commonplace in most home and small-business networks. All of these devices typically have a built-in, basic firewall. This firewall serves as a system's initial line of defense to the Internet. Hackers must get through this firewall to even get to a computer or network. Users who do not have a home or small-business network, or only have one computer, more than likely just plugged into the provided cable, DSL, or Verizon FIOS modem. These also have basic built-in firewalls. Users can have hardware firewalls in addition to their personal firewall, because they are not operating on the same computer or operating system. In most cases, users can employ the default firewall settings with their routers; however, these settings can also be customized to meet specific networking and access needs. All of the following firewalls offer free trial offers with the exception of the Microsoft Windows firewall, which is built into Windows XP Service Pack 2, Windows Vista, and Windows 7.

Microsoft Windows firewall

Windows 7, Vista, and Windows XP (SP2/3) have built-in fire-walls turned on by default. They are accessed via the Control Panel and users have some degree of control over them, though most other personal firewall software is typically more customiz-able. The Windows 7 firewall is significantly improved over XP and Vista and rates overall as a solid personal firewall. In fact, the current version only seems to lack in the notification department, because it does not notify users of potential attacks or network intrusions, which is standard on all other personal firewalls.

The Windows firewall will block outgoing communications that are not allowed and will ask users if they wish to allow them, similar to how other firewalls operate. In Windows 7, users can customize settings for the home network and also customize additional settings to use when they are not on a work or public network, which is ideal for laptop users on the road. One important weakness in the Windows firewall (in all versions) is that it only monitors incoming traffic, not outgoing. If users have malware sending traffic out on their computers, Windows firewall will not detect it, block it, or notify users.

ZoneAlarm Pro Firewall

The ZoneAlarm (**www.zonealarm.com**) OS firewall monitors behaviors within a computer to spot and stop even the most sophisticated new attacks that bypass traditional antiviruses and security suites. It defeats new, advanced attacks like raw-data access, timing, SCM, and COM attacks. It restricts programs from malicious activities, blocking attacks that bypass other defenses. The OS firewall proactively protects against inbound and outbound attacks, making computers invisible to hackers. Additionally, it detects wireless networks and automatically applies the most secure firewall protection setting. ZoneAlarm also provides users with ID protection services and monitors their credit reports daily with e-mail alerts and reports. It automatically analyzes downloads and blocks spyware distribution sites and fraudulent "phishing" Web sites.

Comodo Firewall + Antivirus for Windows

Comodo's firewall (**http://personalfirewall.comodo.com**) blocks suspicious files, stops viruses, and has automatic updates to keep systems fully protected. Comodo provides users basic protection, for free.

Online-Armor

Online-Armor (**www.online-armor.com**) is another free firewall that offers basic protection but does not have automatic updates. The premium edition, Online Armor ++, includes powerful antivirus and antispyware capabilities. Online Armor's personal firewall stops hackers and malicious programs, protects users when banking and transacting online, and protects users' identities.

Sunbelt Personal Firewall

Sunbelt Personal Firewall (**www.sunbeltsoftware.com**) is a robust firewall that protects users from hackers. Recent changes in the program include improvement in network performance, improvement in packet filtering, enhanced process injection, which helps to prevent code injection attempts, and updated intrusion detection rules.

Norman Personal Firewall

Normal Personal Firewall (**www.norman.com**) is a powerful security program that uses computer and port stealth technology to make a computer invisible to hackers. It prevents computers from being implemented in botnets, hijacked, or exposed to other hostile activity. It protects against hackers and malicious Web robots by filtering inbound and outbound traffic. Process hijacking protection detects and reports Trojans and spyware attempting to hijack legitimate applications by inserting malicious code.

OutpostPro Firewall

OutpostPro (**www.agnitum.com**) is an advanced firewall that protects against Web-borne threats. This two-way firewall stops inappropriate or malicious access to a computer from both internal and external sources. It prevents malware from spreading, providing protection against hackers, loss of personal data, unknown malware, and unauthorized program activity.

Network Monitoring Software

Spiceworks

Spiceworks (**www.spiceworks.com**) is an impressive and free network-monitoring package. Spiceworks is a complete network management and monitoring, helpdesk, PC inventory, and software reporting solution used to manage information technology for small and medium businesses.

Outpost Network Security

Outpost Network Security (**www.agnitum.com**) is designed to help small and medium businesses protect against modern security threats. It safeguards local networks against external attacks and internal sabotage, keeps endpoints clean of malware, prevents disclosure of inside information, and polices employee Internet access.

User Activity-Monitoring Software

Spector Pro

Need to monitor the activity of children or employees? Spector Pro (**www.spectorsoft.com**) is an impressive program that records e-mails, chats, IMs, Web sites, Web searches, programs run, keystrokes, files transferred, and screen snapshots. It can even block chats and instant messengers. This program has extensive notification and alerts. It can record MySpace and Facebook activity so users will know everything their kids (or employees) are posting. Users can add online search recording so they know everything users are searching for on Google, Yahoo, AOL, MSN, and Bing.

"Used with permission from SpectorSoft."

"Used with permission from SpectorSoft."

Network Detection and Monitoring (Including Wireless)

PRTG Network Monitor

PRTG Network Monitor (**www.paessler.com**) ensures the availability of network components while also measuring traffic and usage.

WiFi Manager 5

WiFi Manager 5 (**www.manageengine.com**) offers wireless device monitoring, wireless security management, and a variety of reports that remove the complexity of wireless network management. It detects almost all major wireless threats including rogue attacks, intrusions, sniffers, DoS attacks, and vulnerabilities. A free version is available for download and evaluation.

CONCLUSION

This book has been long overdue. There are plenty of other books out there about viruses, malware, hacking, and other threats, but none that address all of these topics and more in one comprehensive guide and offer readers proven solutions and product recommendations to ensure that home and small-business networks are fully protected at all times.

This book is packed with the essentials, and specifically not composed of page after page of content that is either too technically oriented or, quite frankly, unnecessary information. For home computer users and small-business owners, this book should serve as a critical reference in their information technology and security libraries.

Every topic discussed in this book can affect every single computer user. There are millions of victims of spyware, viruses, malware, and other malicious attacks. Many individuals and businesses have lost valuable time, resources, money, and revenue due to viruses, spyware, and malware. The threats are real, and they grow every day. It is absolutely critical that readers follow the guidelines of this book and practice safe Web surfing habits. Users must ensure their operating systems have the latest patches and updates and their computers have active, updated antivirus and antimalware software running at all times. Users need to have a strong personal firewall along with strong passwords to maximize their protection.

Security suites are a good option because they provide protection against a wide variety of threats — including malware, spyware, viruses, and spam — and have extensive tools to protect networks through personal firewalls and network-monitoring tools. Users should consider employing a variety of products, including multiple antispyware and anti-adware products in addition to a strong personal firewall and reputable antivirus package.

Now that you have read this book, and understand the threats you face each time you boot up your computer, are you going to take the steps necessary to protect yourself, your family, and your business?

The increasing numbers of security threats on the Internet certainly make it clear that antivirus software alone will not cut it. To be fair, most modern antivirus software also defends against malware, but this is just the bare minimum needed to defend a computer or network. Viruses, spyware, and malware are quickly morphing into hybrid and previously unknown versions. The threat of botnets, rootkits, and other malicious attacks is very real. Heuristic, behavior-based, and "cloud" technologies are all fighting in the battle against online threats, but winning the war is another matter. The use of targeted attacks or social engineering is becoming much more sophisticated and even savvy Web users are falling prey to this type of attack. The proliferation of social networking sites along with the expansion of Web-enabled smart phones has created an entirely new area of threats. These include identify theft, outside access to personally identifiable information, password theft, and illegal access to financial records. Users should always be on the lookout for changes in their computers, even if they have installed all the protection recommended. Some common signs of malware or infection are a decrease in performance, excessive hard drive activity, new toolbars in Internet browsers, system crashes, changes to the desktop, and changes to a Web browser home page.

Windows 7 is the most secure operating system Microsoft has released, and seems to have won over diehard Windows XP fans who would not make the move to Vista. With all new PCs selling with Windows 7 and many XP and Vista users moving to Windows 7, it will likely be the target of hackers looking for any possible security holes to exploit. Luckily, Microsoft is fast to react and release patches as required, but users must ensure they actually install them onto each of their computers.

Spam will continue to be a constant challenge, growing in volume daily. Spam carries with it viruses, malware, and more, right into users' computers.

Take the time to protect your computer, home network, business computers, and business networks. Use firewalls and good security software to ensure that you are protected as possible and always follow good Web surfing safety habits at all times.

I hope this book has helped to both educate you and arm you with the tools to protect your computers, networks, and assets.

I always look forward to hearing from my readers. If you have any success stories or horror stories you wish to share, feel free to contact me at bruce@brucecbrown.com.

Best Wishes,

Bruce C. Brown

GLOSSARY

ActiveX controls: A set of rules for how software applications share information and execute within Web browsers.

Ad Blocker: Software that prevents unsolicited windows from appearing on a screen or in a browser.

Adware: Software designed to generate intrusive or excessive advertising in a Web browser.

Antispam: Software used to prevent unsolicited e-mail and/or filter it from other e-mail.

Attack: An attempt to bypass security controls on a computer or network for malicious purpose.

Backdoor: An access point through the security of a computer system, network, or software application, deliberately left in place by designers.

Breach: Successful defeat of security controls that results in a malicious penetration of a computer or network, system, application, or server.

Buffer Overflow: An exploitation that alters the flow and functionality of an application by overwriting memory.

Client-Side Scripting: Programming that extends and enhances the functionality of Web pages, typically in JavaScript, JScript, and VBScript.

Common Gateway Interface: A programming standard that allows software to interface and execute applications on Web servers.

Compromise: Intrusion into a computer system, possibly allowing an unauthorized user to access or release sensitive information.

Computer Abuse: Willful, unauthorized activity that might affect the availability or integrity of a computer or network.

Computer Fraud: Crimes involving deliberate misrepresentation or alteration of data to obtain something of value, typically financial in nature.

Computer Network Attack: An attempt to disrupt or destroy information in computers and networks.

Computer Security Intrusion: Unauthorized access of a computer or network.

Computer Worm: A self-replicating software program that spreads over computer networks, often via e-mail.

Content Spoofing: A malicious technique that tricks a user into thinking fake Web site content is an actual, legitimate Web site, usually for purposes of identity theft or financial fraud.

Cookie: A small amount of information sent by the Web server to a Web client that can be stored and retrieved at a later time. In most cases it simply contains identifying information to track user sessions and preferences and recognize return visitors to a Web site.

Cookie Manipulation: The altering or modification of cookie values to exploit security or steal protected information.

Cracker: An individual who breaks computer or network security.

Cracking: The act of breaking into a computer or network.

Crash: An unexpected, immediate failure of a computer (the blue screen of death).

Dark-side Hacker: A malicious hacker.

Demon Dialer: A program that calls the same telephone number over and over again, usually used for a denial of service attack.

Denial of Service: An attack that uses all of a Web server's resources, rendering it unusable for its intended purpose.

DNS Spoofing: Compromising or mimicking a domain name server for a valid domain.

E-Mail Worm: A self-reproducing program that can spread over computer networks, particularly via e-mail; however, it is not attached to another program.

Filename Manipulation: An attack that manipulates URLs and other filenames, causing Web site errors or displaying hidden Web site content or source code.

Firewall: Hardware or software that acts as a gateway between networks and only allows authorized traffic through the wall, providing enhanced security.

Hacker: Someone who attempts to breach security on computers or computer networks through unauthorized access methods.

Hacking: Attempts to circumvent or bypass the security of computers or networks, usually for malicious purposes.

HyperText Transfer Protocol (HTTP): The primary transfer protocol used on the World Wide Web.

Intrusion: Attempts to disrupt or damage the integrity or security of a computer or network.

IP Hijacking: When an unauthorized user intercepts and takes over an established session.

JavaScript: Client-side scripting language that enables dynamic Web page content.

Letterbomb: An e-mail containing live data intended to do malicious damage to a computer or network.

Mailbomb: E-mail encouraging others to send massive amounts of e-mail to an individual e-mail account, with the goal of crashing the recipient's system.

Malware: A term to describe any form of malicious or harmful software, such as viruses, Trojan horses, and spam.

Passive Attack: An attack that monitors and/or views data, without actually damaging it.

Passive Threat: Potential threat of unauthorized disclosure of information without altering or damaging the system and/or data, which nonetheless can be devastating (such as release of credit card data).

Penetration: Successful, unauthorized access into a computer or network.

Pop-up Blocker: A program (or Web browser) that prevents unsolicited windows from opening in a Web browser session.

Replicator: A program that produces copies of itself without any manual intervention, such as worms and viruses.

Retro-Virus: A virus that infects backup copies of data or systems, ensuring it is not possible to recover information using the backup.

Rootkit: Tools that allow a hacker to open a backdoor into a system and steal information or damage/destroy data and functionality.

Scanner: A program that examines systems for potential security vulnerabilities.

Sniffer: A program that can capture passwords, user names, or network data packets for malicious use.

Spam: Unsolicited "junk" e-mail sent to large numbers of people to promote products or services.

Spoofing: Pretending to be someone or something else with malicious intent.

Spyware: Software that monitors activities of a user, without their knowledge and can transmit user activity (keystrokes) elsewhere, typically with malicious intent.

SQL Injection: Exploiting Web sites by altering SQL statements run on the Web server.

SSI Injection: An exploit that allows an attacker to send malicious code into a SQL-based Web application, which is then executed by the Web server.

Trojan Horse: An otherwise innocent-looking program that contains hidden code that can execute, allowing the unauthorized collection, alteration, or destruction of data.

Virus: A program that infects other programs, computers, or networks causing damage or destruction of data or system files. Viruses are typically transmitted via e-mail.

Worm: A program that replicates automatically and travels across the network to infect other computers.

Zombie: A backdoor program that, when installed, waits for instructions from the developer, usually used to steal data from the network or allow unauthorized access.

AUTHOR BIOGRAPHY

Bruce C. Brown is an award-winning author of ten books as well as an active duty Coast Guard officer, where he has served in a variety of assignments for more than 26 years. Bruce is married to Vonda and has three sons: Dalton, Jordan, and Colton. His previous works include:

- *How to Use the Internet to Advertise, Promote, and Market Your Business or Web site with Little or No Money* — Winner: The National 2007 Indie Excellence Book Awards Business Finalist, 2007 Independent Publisher Book Awards Computer/Internet Bronze, ForeWord Magazine's Book of the Year Awards Finalist, USA Best Books Awards 2007 Business: Marketing & Advertising Finalist, Library Journal: Best Business Book 2006 Marketing/Branding

- *The Ultimate Guide to Search Engine Marketing: Pay Per Click Advertising Secrets Revealed* — Winner: USA Best Books Awards 2007 Business: Marketing & Advertising

- *The Complete Guide to E-mail Marketing: How to Create Successful, Spam-free Campaigns to Reach Your Target Audience and Increase Sales*

- *Complete Guide to Google Advertising: Including Tips, Tricks, & Strategies to Create a Winning Advertising Plan*

- *The Secret Power of Blogging: How to Promote and Market Your Business, Organization, or Cause With Free Blogs* — Winner: Florida Publishers Association 2009 President's Book Award (Silver Medal - Business)

- *Returning From the War on Terrorism: What Every Veteran Needs to Know to Receive Your Maximum Benefits*

- *The Complete Guide to Affiliate Marketing on the Web: How to Use and Profit from Affiliate Marketing Programs*

- *Google Income: How Anyone of Any Age, Location, and/or Background Can Build a Highly Profitable Online Business with Google*

- *How to Open and Operate a Financially Successful Web-Based Business*

- *How to Build Your Own Web Site With Little or No Money: The Complete Guide for Business and Personal Use*

He holds degrees from Charter Oak State College and the University of Phoenix. He currently splits his time between Land O' Lakes, Florida and Miami, Florida.

BIBLIOGRAPHY

Audit My PC. Audit My PC, 2009. Web. Dec 2009.

Browser Security Test. Scanit, 2009. Web. Dec 2009.

Emsisoft. Emsisoft, 2009. Web. Dec 2009.

Eset. Eset, 2009. Web. Dec 2009.

Firetrust. Firetrust, 2009. Web. Dec 2009.

Google Webmaster Central. Google, Inc., 2009. Web. Dec 2009.

Microsoft. Microsoft, 2009. Web. Dec 2009.

Norton Security. Symantec Corporation , 2009. Web. Dec 2009.

Panda Security. Panda Security USA, 2009. Web. Dec 2009.

SonicWALL. SonicWALL, 2009. Web. Dec 2009.

SPAMfighter. SPAMfighter, 2009. Web. Dec 2009.

Trend Micro. Trend Micro, 2009. Web. Dec 2009.

INDEX